THE INTERNATIONAL BACCALAUREATE DIPLOMA PROGRAM AND THE SCHOOL LIBRARY

THE INTERNATIONAL BACCALAUREATE DIPLOMA PROGRAM AND THE SCHOOL LIBRARY

Inquiry-Based Education

ANTHONY TILKE

 LIBRARIES UNLIMITED

AN IMPRINT OF ABC-CLIO, LLC
Santa Barbara, California • Denver, Colorado • Oxford, England

Library of Congress Cataloging-in-Publication Data

Tilke, Anthony.
  The International Baccalaureate Diploma Program and the School Library:
Inquiry-Based Education / Anthony Tilke.
    p. cm
  Includes bibliographical references and index.
    ISBN 978-1-59884-641-6 (pbk.: acid-free paper);   ISBN 978-1-59884-642-3 (ebook)
    1. School libraries.   2. International baccalaureate.   3. School librarian participation in curriculum planning.   4. Inquiry-based learning.   5. International education.
6. Internationalism.   7. Education and globalization.   I. Title.
    Z675.S3T483   2011
    027.8'223—dc22   2010051624

ISBN: 978-1-59884-641-6; EISBN: 978-1-59884-642-3
15   14   13   12   11   1   2   3   4   5

This book is also available on the World Wide Web as an eBook.
Visit www.abc-clio.com for details.

Libraries Unlimited
An Imprint of ABC-CLIO, LLC

ABC-CLIO, LLC
130 Cremona Drive, P.O. Box 1911
Santa Barbara, California 93116-1911

This book is printed on acid-free paper ∞

Manufactured in the United States of America

CONTENTS

1 Introduction   1

2 The International Baccalaureate Diploma
   Programme and the IB   9

3 The IBDP Subject Matrix and Core Features   21

4 The Extended Essay   33

5 The IB Learner Profile and Academic Honesty   47

6 How Do IBDP Students Use the School Library?   57

7 Teachers, Administrators, and the Librarian in the IBDP   71

8 A Consumer-Focused School Library   81

9 Roles of the IBDP Library and Librarian   87

Appendixes

   Appendix 1: Theory of Knowledge Resources for a School Library   97
   Appendix 2: Examples of Library Information for Help-sheets
               and Library Websites   103
   Appendix 3: Example of Library Booklist to Support Group 1   109
   Appendix 4: Information Literacy–Related Research
               Concerning the IBDP   111
   Appendix 5: Books on Essay Writing, the Extended
               Essay, and Abstracts   115
   Appendix 6: Example of a Policy on Donation of IBDP
               Extended Essays to the School Library   117
   Appendix 7: Glossary of IB Acronyms and Terminology   119

References   121

Index   131

1

———•◦※◦•———

INTRODUCTION

Important new ways of working in the 21st century—such as thinking creatively and across traditional disciplines, as using skills in relating to and cooperating with people, employing a different definition of being literate, and being smarter or thinking critically about information—were some of the things that Claudia Wallis and Sonja Steptoe, reporting in *Time* magazine in 2006, thought were necessary for students to learn and use in this century. They considered that the International Baccalaureate Diploma Programme (often referred to as the IBDP; the spelling of *programme* is explained later) would be an excellent curriculum to follow, so that students could develop these vital aptitudes and skills. This curriculum, the IBDP, based as it is on inquiry and self-discovery and offering breadth and depth, poses challenges and offers rewards for schools and their communities—students, teachers, administrators, and, of course, librarians.

The International Baccalaureate (IB) as an organization, with its three curricular programs, is a developing presence in and among educational thinkers and school systems worldwide. This is also true of the IBDP, which is growing in the United States and also in other globally important countries such as India and China. The IBDP was introduced in the 1970s, initially in international schools, so that children of diplomats, businesspeople, those in the armed forces, and officials in nongovernmental organizations (NGOs), and other expatriates living abroad, could experience a rigorous curriculum that would enable them to gain entry to universities in their home countries and indeed other countries. Now, the IBDP has spread throughout the world and is offered not only in international schools but also in public (state-funded) as well as private or independent sector schools. The IB website notes that, in 2010, "The IB Americas [region of the IB, known as IBA] includes IB World Schools in 31 countries and territories in Central, North and South America. IB World Schools in the Americas are state/public, private, magnet, charter, international, parochial and secular and serve a broad and diverse range of students in urban, suburban and rural communities. There are . . . 1,123 [schools] providing the Diploma Programme in 30 countries" in the IBA region alone (International Baccalaureate Organization [IBO], 2010a). Globally, there are nearly 2,200 schools offering the diploma. In terms of the IBDP, the Americas region is the largest, followed by Europe, Africa and the Middle East, and the Asia–Pacific regions (IBO, 2010a).

When one college applied to the IB in order to teach the IBDP, some practitioners at the institution noted that it succeeded because the faculty had the "right educational experience, and the library met the IBDP's academic demands," though what the latter requirements actually were remained unidentified (Andain, Rutherford, & Allen, 2006, p. 62). Indeed, official documentation specifically about the role of the school library in the IBDP is limited, which is partly why librarians and others tend to ask questions like: "How do I support the program?" and "What is my role and that of the library in the IBDP?" As a response, this book narrates the impact of a school library on one school's IBDP community, students, and teachers and also provides a range of theoretical and practical strategies that a school librarian can use to develop the school library program to support the IBDP. The book provides information for those embarking on the IBDP, especially as there are regular pleas from new or novice IBDP librarians on various listservs for direction, support, and ideas. There should also be enough detail (such as research findings and report of good practice) for more experienced librarians. The book should also be capable of being read by interested nonlibrarians, such as administrators, because their role in comprehending, articulating, and supporting a role for the school library within the IBDP is, in a way, almost more important than that of librarians.

Addressing heads of IB schools in Geneva in 1995, one librarian described the IBDP as offering a "research approach to learning, rather than the mere accumulation of factual knowledge" and indicated that "when our students go on to university . . . they are likely to find a complex library . . . which can be very daunting. Preparing students for university should include preparing them to be confident library users" (Clark, 1995, p. 43). Research and inquiry are therefore seen to be integral to pursuing the IBDP successfully. As late as 2005, there was little if any published research work about the library and librarian and the IBDP—although there are some professional writing and self-help local or regional support groups as well as official and unofficial listservs or online groups—but it is not uncommon to see repeated requests for information from aspirant IBDP schools and their librarians for *any* information about what is required in terms of effective library support and how to obtain it.

This book therefore blends academic knowledge, practical strategies, and insight about the IBDP. It is based on the present writer's background, which comprises the following:

1. Over 10 years experience of the IBDP in four different international schools
2. Experience as an IB library workshop leader in the IB Asia–Pacific region and as chair of the International Baccalaureate Asia–Pacific Library and Information Specialists (IBAPLIS) group
3. Doctoral research with Charles Sturt University, Australia, concerning the impact of an international school library on the IBDP
4. Six years' experience as a Theory of Knowledge (TOK) teacher in the IBDP, simultaneously serving as an IB examiner for the TOK essay
5. Work as full-time school and youth library adviser with the U.K. Library Association (as it then was, but is now called the Chartered Institute of

Library and Information Professionals, or CILIP) in London, which involved work in promoting a library role when the then government looked at adopting a baccalaureate model for the national education system

It is also important to recognize that the IB community of librarians, abstract and fragmented as it may be in practice (but only because it is worldwide), is a very helpful and cooperative one, and that good practice and new ideas are shared by various librarians, often online, but also through IB training events for librarians. The reader will find that effective practices from various practitioners are reflected in the book.

This introduction naturally deals with various broader issues about the IBDP and also some basic ideas, concepts, and questions related to school librarianship. These are presented in this introduction to set the scene and arrive at some common understandings.

What is a school library? This seems the most obvious concept of all and perhaps superfluous to question; however, if you ask members of your school community what *they* think their school library exists for, several (possibly conflicting) answers or viewpoints may be forthcoming. These may help to explain use and nonuse patterns and issues that may have occurred for the library in your school. For whatever reason, the position statements of the library and information science (LIS) sector on the role of school libraries nevertheless see the need to define what a school library is. In Australia, a school library includes space, facilities—not least information and communications technology (ICT)—and staff to facilitate services or a library program (Australian School Library Association & Australian Library and Information Association, 2001). Guidelines in the United Kingdom for CILIP promote the idea of providing "a learning space . . . as its principal purpose" (Barrett & Douglas, 2004, p. 24). Are these definitions different from American Association of School Librarians (AASL) documentation? To whom is the LIS community providing definitions? Are the definitions communicated effectively, and are they agreed upon?

What is a school librarian? The definition of this role may only further confuse matters, as what constitutes a librarian in a school varies from country to country and, in some cases, within a country. Even school library literature uses several terms and acknowledges variations. Terms are important, as a given term may affect how people see and perceive the school librarian. There is some research to suggest that, for all the variations around the world, there is no research-proven "best" type of school librarian in terms of terminology, education, and experience (Turner, 2007). Nevertheless, for clarity and comprehensiveness, this book uses the term *librarian*.

What is a baccalaureate? A baccalaureate-style education offers a holistic approach to knowledge and education for pretertiary education students. There are several models, but probably the best known is the IBDP (Phillips & Pound, 2003). One reason that the IBDP is the best known is probably that it is offered worldwide rather than in only one geographical area.

What could be the impact of a school library on the IBDP and the various groups of people involved: students, parents, teachers, administrators, and the IB itself? This question was at the heart of research undertaken by the present writer and is discussed in this book, but taken more generally, there is no shortage of research and even more professional or secondary literature in the school library sector that promotes the idea of educational change, life-enhancing skills, and meaningful knowledge acquisition by students. However, an interesting question is how accurately more general educational research and professional literature may reflect such a premise in relation to the IBDP. Perhaps IB school libraries and the curriculum itself are so different that it is difficult to apply existing LIS research to such a setting, or perhaps there is more synergy. This question, too, is reflected in the book.

How useful are impact studies and evidence-based research? Proponents of research about school libraries maintain that using impact studies and evidence-based research or practice is better than using unsubstantiated advocacy (perhaps including guidelines and recommended role statements) to policymakers and school administrators (Todd, 2006). However, especially as regards earlier research, say before 1995, these studies started and ended with a library point of view, with the aim of justifying input measures. Indeed, a belief paradigm based on the social good of libraries was the premise of some studies (Streatfield & Markless, 1994). The present writer's review of literature relating to impact studies of school libraries showed a clear geographical division of quantitative and qualitative studies—quantitative ones tended to occur in North America, whereas qualitative ones featured in literature related mainly to the United Kingdom and Australia. Initially, impact studies were used for advocacy purposes. Although evidence-based practice (EBP) informed or improved practice, the two styles now seem more mixed. Larger-scale studies, more typically associated with the United States, based any impact on test score results. They tended to identify a roughly 8 percent factor for school library impact in high schools, whereas up to 50 percent difference may be due to socioeconomic factors overall. Such studies have typically been promoted to policymakers in terms that would suggest the causal nature of any impact. Smaller studies, typically qualitative in nature, tended not to relate the impact of a school library to test scores but rather to broader aspects of learning, such as literacy, reading, and confidence (e.g., Williams & Wavell, 2001, 2002). However, a large study in Ohio (Todd & Kuhlthau, 2005a,b) looked both quantitatively and qualitatively at how students of a wide age range were helped by the school library.

How useful are qualitative methods to research on school libraries? Are such methods better than or just different from quantitative methods? There are different views about the equal validity of quantitative and qualitative methods of research; some of these may reflect realpolitik reasons. However, in terms of detail and identifying specific situations, it is generally considered that the qualitative method may allow expressions of views, feelings, and values to be effectively identified. For the study that forms the focus of this book, the qualitative method was chosen, as the study wanted to find out what the stakeholders in the IBDP—students, teachers, administrators, and librarians—thought about the role of the library in support of the IBDP. To further enable this to be achieved, the particular qualitative methodology adopted in the study was grounded theory, or, in other words, theory that arises from the data during the research process and is grounded in such data and in the research experiences of the researcher, rather than a hypothesis "being imposed on the research" at the beginning of the research process (Bartlett, Burton, & Peim, 2001, p. 46). There is a relationship with ethnography, so that studies are associated with detailed accounts of the actions, thoughts, and views of specific groups of people. In such studies, including the present study, appropriate and relevant techniques include extensive observation as well as interviewing (with analysis of each line of verbatim transcripts), thus allowing for rich narratives of specific situations (Charmaz, 2006). The values, feelings, and views of particular students, teachers, and administrators therefore inform this book to a considerable degree. Because articulated and perceived views and values could have been different had other people been studied, grounded theory methodology cannot claim to be generalizable. Nevertheless, any application of the study's findings rests with the reader, and it is the reflection process on similarities or otherwise with the reader's own situation that will be valuable. Indeed, such a process probably needs to happen whatever the methodology chosen. (Interestingly, grounded theory is chosen more and more often for qualitative LIS studies and has also been used for some of the IBDP studies from North America that are cited in this book.)

A great deal of research is available from various countries, not least in the English-speaking world, concerning school libraries, both in general and relating to older students, though not about IBDP libraries specifically. This book identifies relevant, valid research, irrespective of country, making links and contrasting with the IBDP as appropriate. Given that the IBDP is an international curriculum, it is apposite to cite literature internationally. Some studies about relevant aspects of the IBDP are each cited several times in the text; for convenience, these studies and short descriptions of their main features are listed in Appendix 4.

How relevant is internationalism? Because it is included in the title of the curriculum, *internationalism* is very much a key term and concept, although the preferred term is *international mindedness*. One of the questions librarians tend to ask (and should ask) in relation to the IBDP is "How do we try to ensure that our libraries are international minded in outlook?" However, there are various definitions of *internationalism*, a term that can be ambiguous (Cambridge & Thompson, 2004). Nevertheless, internationalism has connections with international schools, which exist in many countries of the world, and also with the IBDP as an example of an international academic curriculum. However, international mindedness is not limited to international schools but can be applied to any school context. It is therefore a key idea, and is discussed more in the next chapter.

How extensive will inquiry be in the IBDP? Inquiry, as a curriculum stance, pervades all IB programs. It will look different in the IBDP partly because of the prescribed content in subject syllabuses and, more importantly, the ways of learning and teaching preferred by subject faculty members and how the core requirements work in individual schools. All these will play a part in how inquiry looks in the IBDP and how much of it is seen in the library and by the librarian. Although the inquiry or research models that librarians are familiar with could well be relevant, remember that "one model doesn't fit all." Thus advocating these models may not work in every subject area, although some educational writers on concepts, understanding, essential questions, and inquiry are highly regarded in the IB world. This very much includes the Understanding by Design concept developed by Wiggins and McTighe (2005, 2007).

How much should technology drive the direction of an IBDP library? It shouldn't. Relevant and useful technology will naturally be used and, as an information specialist, an IB librarian will continually be looking for ways in which information, perceived knowledge, and ideas can be obtained in whatever format or media. In a similar way, the IB itself is looking at ways in which technology can be harnessed in the interest of its programs. Nevertheless, IB programs are used throughout the world and it would be impossible to require specific levels of ICT and particular products, because what might be available and possible in one part of the world wouldn't necessarily be found in another. Realistically though, in some parts of the world, a technology-rich school library is a given, yet it is not automatically so, even in any one country. Although the use of technology is of course discussed, when and where relevant, in various areas of this book, the main emphasis is on the curriculum and the needs of an IB school community.

Terminology and acronyms. Education and library worlds abound with acronyms and terminology or jargon, which may be specific to their own paradigm. An example from the LIS world is *information literacy*, which is a common enough term to librarians, though does not enjoy synergy amongst members of subject faculties. The text of a book that seeks to blend the two worlds of education and librarianship is likely to be rich in specific terms and acronyms, but which nevertheless may be commonly understood. Acronyms are also used in relation to the IBDP, and, to aid clarity, a glossary of IB terms is appended to this book. Readers may also wish to look for a more comprehensive glossary of IB terms, which is available on the IB website. A URL is not given for this page, as of course it may change, but more importantly because it is a very good strategy for the school librarian to be familiar with the public IB website and what is commonly referred to as the OCC (Online Curriculum Center), which is maintained by the organization for educators.

One word, though, about the use of the acronym IB. In 2007, the International Baccalaureate Organization (IBO) decided to brand itself more simply and calls itself International Baccalaureate, which is a registered name, although the website remains www.ibo.org. A number of writers and practitioners have always referred to the IB, and they might mean the organization itself or its first curriculum—that is, the IBDP. As this program existed on its own for over 20 years (before being joined by primary and middle-years programs), it also tended to be called simply IB, and the terms were regarded as being synonymous. Finally, should the word be spelled *program* or *programme*? Because the IB uses the latter spelling, this has been preserved where the full formal title is given, titles of IB documents given, and quotations are made.

How is the book organized? More general and perhaps basic information and discussion about important aspects of the IBDP will be found towards the beginning of the book. Chapters blend information and strategies, but each chapter ends with a summary of practical strategies for the librarian. As the book progresses, there is more presentation of the narratives of those involved in the study, upon which this book is partly based, and which includes discussion of the academic research and findings of the present study.

PRACTICAL STRATEGIES FOR THE LIBRARIAN

- Librarians should become familiar with the IB's public website and OCC, which is available as a tab through www.ibo.org. (To access the OCC, password and codes are required and should be obtainable from the school's IBDP coordinator.)

- As an information specialist, becoming familiar with the contents of the IB website could be an enabling role for the librarian, especially in schools that are beginning to look at adopting the IBDP, so that the librarian could inform or advise faculty colleagues who are looking for information about various aspects of the IBDP.

- Seek clarity in your school regarding understanding of the role of the school library, which may involve revisiting or developing written policy statements.
- Think about impact and evidence-based research in relation to the school library. Especially, be aware of what the purpose of research is and who it is aimed at.
- Find or develop a definition of internationalism and try to relate it to your library.
- Think about the jargon, terminology, and acronyms that are commonly used in school librarianship. Do we use it in our school situations, and is it understandable by our school community?

2

THE INTERNATIONAL BACCALAUREATE DIPLOMA PROGRAMME AND THE IB

Established in 1970, the IBDP started in international schools around the world, for which it was originally designed, to meet the perceived needs and aspirations of children of expatriates. The IBO supports and develops the IBDP, but since approximately the mid-1990s, there are also two other curriculums. These are the Primary Years Programme (PYP) and the Middle Years Programme (MYP), which together with the IBDP, provide a continuum of K–12 international education. However, the diploma is different from both the PYP and MYP. The latter are both curriculum frameworks, so schools can develop their own content, whereas the IBDP contains prescribed content and assessment, in order to comply with requirements for student entry into tertiary education systems around the world. A basic guide, which is sometimes referred to as a monograph about the IBDP, is called *The Diploma Programme: A Basis for Practice*. Although issued in 2002, the latest version is available on the IB website and provides useful background information about the IBDP. (There is also a document about the IB continuum, again available on the IB website.)

Schools may offer one, two, or three IB programs; it is not uncommon for a school to have a different (such as a national or state) curriculum until students reach 16 years of age, and then offer the IBDP, either as an option amongst other courses (e.g., AP) or as the main or sole curriculum offered to 16- to 18-year-old students, which is the typical age of IBDP candidates (as students may be referred to in IB documents). Nevertheless, the continuum of international education is very important in and to IB philosophy, and schools that offer the three programs are now referred to as Continuum Schools. Many documents issued by the IB that relate to their key concepts, such as the Learner Profile, academic honesty, and internationalism, are applicable to all three IB programs, not just one. So, even if your school is offering one program, such as the IBDP, it is nevertheless important to be aware of the philosophies behind the IB "big ideas," not only to understand the educational theory underpinning the programs, but also to make practical connections, such as understanding the "concluding projects" as each program ends with a student project—in the case of the IBDP, this is, of course, the extended essay.

As an overall concept, the IBDP offers "breadth" through subject groups and "coherence" through TOK and "[through the extended essay] writing, analytical and research skills far beyond what is usually asked of a student in high school" (Sjogren & Vermey, 1986, p. 27). Indeed, it is this core of the IBDP (which features TOK, the extended essay, and creativity, action, and service [known as CAS]), which is regarded as a unique feature of the IBDP, and distinguishes it from other baccalaureate models. There are other models. The IBDP is merely one, though it is a prominent and probably the best-known one (Hayden & Thompson, 1995). Le Metais (2002) suggested, in a document published by the U.K. National Foundation for Educational Research, that the IBDP is increasingly viewed as a model for national curricula and national school systems. While there is a perception that the IBDP is offered mainly in wealthy, private schools, Cambridge and Thompson (2004) found that half the schools that offered IBDP were actually those in the state or public sector. Therefore the model is important, and a wide variety of schools offer the program. By extension, they are supported by school libraries that are different in setting, size, funding, and staffing.

There is also a perception that the IBDP is more suited for some gifted students (e.g., Buchanan, Douglas, Hachlaf, Varner, & Williams, 2005), but there are examples of it being offered for whole multiple-ability year groups (Rataj-Worsnop, 2003). The view that the IBDP is purely for gifted students is not one that the IB itself necessarily shares. Indeed, in a study in three high schools in the United States, Kyburg, Hertberg-Davis, and Callahan (2007) looked at minority students' experiences of the IBDP and AP. The study showed that it was important that students had a strong belief in their ability to succeed in the diploma, and that scaffolding to support such students was necessary. Specific support was also a key factor when Burris, Welner, Wiley, and Murphy (2007) looked at how the IBDP was extended within a school district in New York. (Both were broader educational studies; however, there was nevertheless no mention of the role of a librarian, which was surprising given that the studies looked at scaffolding support for students.) Again, this has implications for libraries, as the finance, expertise, and time commitments needed by librarians to support the IBDP may also be required to be balanced with other, perhaps competing, needs and programs.

For each subject taken, IBDP students complete written assignments and coursework, which is assessed both by teachers of the school concerned and external examiners (who are invariably teachers in other IB schools). Assignments include developed pieces of writing that should or could involve research, such as an essay for TOK and the extended essay.

A certificate option also exists where students follow courses and sit examinations in subjects only, and do not undertake the core elements of the IBDP. A further, more recent, development is towards creating more vocational or practical subject areas, rather than just sticking with the existing academic subjects. As online options are also being developed, there are many options and planned changes within the overall IBDP concept.

What have students gained by choosing the IBDP? A survey of IB students from two schools in British Columbia, Canada, indicated that they found it was hard work, but recognized and valued peer, teacher, and family support; they learned time management and organization skills, developed a firm work ethic, communicated better, developed critical thinking skills, and broadened their view of the world (Buchanan et al., 2005). Another study of gifted female students—albeit a small IB sample—found that the support of and rapport with teachers was vital, but that students focused on memorizing a considerable amount of content, rather than necessarily understanding the content. Students also relied on other students, and one "specifically mentioned that she often went to the library to study for her classes with a group of friends" (Vanderbrook, 2006, p. 143). This was the main comment about the school library in this study.

So, although there is potential for school library support and involvement in the IBDP, it really depends on how the program is developed at a particular school, how teachers teach it, and how students learn. Each school will (usually) be different. Librarians will look in vain for officially sanctioned stand-alone guidelines or developed statements about the role of the school library from the IB, but it is more important to look at two key documents and the in-school processes that these documents identify. Both processes and resulting school documentation should include contributions from the library and its librarian. The relevant IB documents are the *Guide to Programme Evaluation* and the *Programme Standards and Practices.* (On the IB website, you may also find helpful information in a Power-Point presentation from 2007 called "Diploma Programme Evaluation" by staff of the IB, Stephen Keegan, and Stuart Jones.)

Because documents relating to and regulating the IBDP are revised regularly, it is vital to refer to the latest edition. These may be found on the IB website, either on the public site or on the OCC. The IBDP coordinator at the school will also have knowledge of these documents and their location, and be able to advise on current versions.

GUIDE TO PROGRAMME EVALUATION

In order to become authorized to offer the IB programs, individual schools need to complete a self-evaluation, which will include reference to important school documentation and policies together with a reflection on philosophy, school organization, curriculum, and students. It is worthwhile for a librarian to read this guide and discuss with the IBDP coordinator where the library fits in, which library documents and policies are needed, and so on. The school self-evaluation is submitted to the relevant IB regional office that will depute a group of teachers who have been trained in the IB authorization process to consider and respond to the school's application.

IBDP schools are re-authorized every five years, and a self-study process is required each time. The relevant IB regional office responds to each self-study report. As part of the process, there may be a specific form to be completed by the librarian, though, in the past, this has varied depending on the exact requirements of the regional office concerned. Again, the school's IBDP coordinator will know the exact requirements. As an example, this is the response by a librarian to two standard questions that concern the library in the resources section for the self-evaluation process of the IBDP re-authorization of one school. This proforma asks a standard question about changes in the school during a five year period that would relate directly to the teaching of the IBDP and the learning experiences of diploma students. The form specifically mentions the library, technology support and infrastructure, learning materials, and so on.

- *In 2000, the main high school building, including classrooms, laboratories, IT centre and Library were refurbished. A new, expanded IT centre was created and the Library was re-planned (including facilities for grade 11 and 12 students on study-hall). A recording studio was also created. [Other information followed, including]*
- *In 2003, Internet access was improved with the provision of laptop computers and strategic provision of hubs in various parts of the school . . .*

And a specific question about library use:

Q. How does the school use the library and other resources to support learning and research [with regard to the IB Diploma]?

Subject departments use the library to varying degrees. Some assume that the library will provide study space, reference material, and appropriate magazines to support student students. Some departments use the library for specific research-based assignments. Again, some teachers are proactive in recommending resources for the library. All students have study halls (periods) and are encouraged to study in the library, under the supervision of the librarian. One strategy to develop the library role has been to appoint the librarian to be coordinator for Extended Essays.

When one U.S. high school introduced the IBDP about 15 years ago, they identified resource needs in relation to library provision, and developed a three-year library budget plan involving $15,000 in total, in order to improve the library collection and information services. However, in this school, the IBDP was an option along with other courses, and the school aimed to make library resources purchased to support IBDP needs available to the wider school population, especially as concerned ICT products, such as subscription databases. Internet provision was also increased (in a pre-wireless environment). Such an inclusive ideal applied to the library facility as a whole, and IB and non-IB students were treated equally. However, it was noted that, in order to increase the "level of research to community college standards, volumes of historical writings were added and literary criticism was updated. Because 95% of our extended essays are written in history or language A English, regular additions are imperative" (Chris, 1999, p. 34).

A group of teachers in British Columbia undertook a research project to look at resource implications of the IBDP. They indicated that a library needed to be provided and had a large role in the IBDP. Though no further details were given, the focus of the research being with resource inputs, they noted a lack of literature about resource implications of the diploma. They issued a survey about school wide resourcing issues to find out what school stakeholders thought. The survey asked parents and teachers in two schools whether library resources (specifically periodicals and books) were sufficient for the IBDP. Teachers thought the library resources were sufficient, though they thought laptop access was insufficient. A clear parent view did not come out of the research, though those parents that answered the question thought that more library resources were needed, and one parent specifically mentioned an additional library post. Because the teachers found there was uncertainty surrounding what is needed for IBDP, they recommended that the IB develop a list of resources—building, staff, materials—that a school needed when applying to offer the IBDP (Buchanan et al., 2005).

One IBDP practitioner has outlined possible library expectations from an IBO authorization team, insisting that the library "is a major focus" for such teams. It is important, therefore, that teams find the library to contain nonfiction materials that are accessible in appropriate quantity and quality by students. In this assessment, the library environment is also important; it should be housed in a "spacious and inviting area conducive to study and research." As well as adequate Internet access, the collection, in addition to information books, should include periodicals and fiction that is "representative of the nationalities of the school, in particular to support the language A1 courses." It is likely that many schools require some pre-authorization funding and "some schools have spent US$10–20,000 and more on their libraries for authorization, but a well-stocked library" may need less seed funding (Jones, 2004a, p. 41).

IB as a curriculum organization clearly values opportunities for students to benefit from the provision—through school libraries—for opportunities for research and inquiry about other languages and internationalism, whether in print form or through technology. Students should be stimulated or energized in their learning experiences through using a well-stocked school library that is added to and updated regularly in the framework of a clear and ongoing budgetary process, which indicates administration support and involvement.

There is a *School Guide to the Authorization* visit specifically for the IBDP. The latest version is dated 2006, but again, please check the IB website for the latest version (it is available on the public site). The document is available through pages that are IB region specific, so exact procedure and detail may vary with the IB region concerned. This document gives detail about what is involved in an initial authorization visit, what the team will typically do, and who they will meet. It specifically mentions librarians. In fact, there is a small section headed "Librarians, Counselors and Non-teaching Staff," which indicates that—typically—authorization teams should look at how librarians and other categories of staff will be involved and what their exact role is. Specifically, it questions whether there is a professional librarian in the school and prompts teams to inquire into how librarians will work with IBDP teachers and students. This indicates that the school needs to have thought about these aspects rather than obtain received wisdom, as it were, from the IB.

Once a school has been authorized to offer one or more IB programs, it is referred to as an IB World School.

PROGRAMME STANDARDS AND PRACTICES

The relevant IB edition was issued in November 2010, and replaces the version from 2005. The latest version is effective from the beginning of 2011. This document identifies standards to which a school should work towards. One of the changes between the editions is that that 2005 document indicated that standards were applicable to all three IB programs, though each standard generally included program-specific practices. Previously, standards were grouped by four headings: philosophy, school organization, curriculum, and students. Now, there are three headings: philosophy, organization, and curriculum. This is an example of how IB documents change over the years, so it is vital that the librarian consults the most current document. It is worthwhile for the librarian to look at these program-specific practices aims or targets and identify where the library can contribute. As far as the new standards are concerned, these are discussed in more detail in the final chapter.

INTERNATIONALISM AND LANGUAGE IN THE IBDP

The key IB document that discusses internationalism is *Towards a Continuum of International Education*. This document explains a pedagogical approach and assessment, with good levels of overview of the IBDP in particular. There are some related terms about which it is helpful to be aware. Amongst the more important are globalization and also third culture kids (TCK). TCK describes a student who moves from one culture to another culture, and is educated in a third culture. This term has been regarded typically as relating to students in international schools, but its use is not limited to such students (Pollock & Van Reken, 2009). The term may also arise, for instance, when such students go to universities in a third country (Van Reken & Quick, 2010). An aspect of this—though it is also a main feature of IB programs—is that a student may learn in a second or third language, and not the language spoken at home. Therefore, another important document written and published by the IB is called *Learning in a Language Other Than Mother Tongue in IB Programmes* (2008).

When thinking about how best to develop a school library collection suitable to IBDP, it is important to be aware of internationalism or international mindedness and make sure the collection reflects this concept. Authorization teams may wish to be reassured that international mindedness has been considered in relation to the library collection. This may be achieved by including publications from different countries; authors who represent different cultures; and information about different cultures, arts, lifestyles, economics, politics, and ways of living. An international emphasis should be utilized in both fiction and nonfiction areas. This may include narratives of people who go to different cultures and help people in different ways.

One way of developing international mindedness is to ask other librarians for suggestions. Librarians on one international school listserv started a thread on this topic, for instance, and came up with a varied list of titles. A modern classic example would be the famous book about developing education in an Asian country, *Three Cups of Tea* by Greg Mortenson. Other suggestions were: *The Geography of Thought: How Asians and Westerners Think Differently, and Why* (Richard Nisbett); *The Culture Code* (Clotaire Rapaille); *The New Asian Hemisphere* (Kishore Mahbubani); and *What the World Eats* (Peter Menzel). These and other titles have been tagged as a global reading list for high school by an American IB librarian working at the United World College of South-East Asia, Singapore, on http://www.worldcat.org (Day, 2010).

To go deeper into cultures, it could be helpful to look at how we understand different cultures. IB documentation refers to an iceberg model, whereby we can readily see some elements in a culture. These easily seen elements could be considered to be above the water line of an iceberg, and in our metaphor, the less obvious elements are there, but they are below the water line. Can we identify such ideas/concepts that are not so readily identifiable, and, if so, is it possible to represent these in the library collection?

It is also helpful to look at language provision in the school library. Are curriculum, community and mother tongue, or home first language collections maintained in the library, or are all library resources offered in English or one language only?

If your school library uses the Dewey Decimal Classification, it might be helpful to look at the classification for literatures. Is the separation of literatures by language helpful? In terms of looking at world literature (which is an approach taken in one of the subject areas of the IBDP), consider the average size of an 800s collection: does the classification make it easier for students to find materials? Remember that students are accustomed to finding material by simply clicking on a link on a screen. One approach to make it easier for student to find world literature texts could be to merge all the English language numbers (e.g., American literature, English literature, Caribbean English literature, etc.). An information sheet for students, which explains such an approach, is included at Appendix 2.

Indeed, it might be also helpful to look at the variety of English language publications in your library. Naturally, there are now many co-editions, and publishing houses are more international, to the extent that a number are owned by multinational conglomerates. Nevertheless, it may be helpful to look at your collection to identify the balance of North American English language titles with, say, Australasian English, British English, Caribbean English, and titles published in English from South America and India, for example. The inclusion of such titles may just give a subtle difference of perspective or point of view, which can help make a library collection more international in focus.

Another aspect where the library can make a contribution or impact is by making available a live and relevant collection of materials for the professional development of the faculty. In terms of the present discussion, such a collection should include material on internationalism and international education, language development, bilingualism, TCK, and so on. Along with academic texts, it is important to remember the *Journal of Research in International Education* (a periodical that owes its genesis earlier this century from input from the IB), a subscription to which will include electronic access to previous issues. The comprehensive bibliography in the *Towards a Continuum of International Education* document would be a good starting point for recommendations on how to develop a collection for educators about aspects of international education.

WHAT IS THE IB, AND HOW IS IT ORGANIZED?

The IB is a worldwide organization whose remit is explained in its mission statement, which appears on the front of each IB document. The IB aims to "develop inquiring, knowledgeable and caring young people who help to create a better and more peaceful world through intercultural understanding and respect." The IB cooperates with various partners, such as schools, as well as various international organizations and national governments to develop curricula that are focused on international education, challenging, and rigorously assessed. The IB has a vision for students who experience IB programs: they should be "active, compassionate and lifelong learners" who, crucially, "understand that other people with their differences, can also be right." This is all in the mission statement, and librarians are encouraged to read it verbatim and reflect on how their library could contribute. The mission statement is fundamental to understanding what the IB is about. Students and student outcomes, not least inquiry (a term which is specifically mentioned in the first sentence of the mission statement), are at the center of the IB's activity.

The IB has offices in North America and Europe and elsewhere in the world. The headquarters are in Geneva, Switzerland, thus showing its European origins; however, it is firmly a global organization, organized on a regional basis. The current regions are the Americas (IBA); Europe, the Middle East, and Africa (IBEAM); and Asia-Pacific (IBAP). There may be offices in countries within a particular region as well as a regional office. There is a curriculum and assessment center (IBCA), currently in Cardiff, Wales, United Kingdom, but it will be moving to the Hague in the Netherlands. This is an important office for the IBDP; the staff provides expert advice about the program, and examination and regulations information.

The IB also coordinates a network of examiners, who are typically IB teachers in schools around the world, and regionally supports trained IB workshop leaders and those involved in program evaluation teams, who again are teachers in schools. Workshops are an important professional development tool of the IB, as each teacher involved in IB programs needs to be trained, invariably through workshops that are either offered or approved by the IB, and which are delivered in various levels or categories (1–3), with varying content to reflect the experience of the participant. Whilst a conference is also offered in each region on an annual basis, the main regular method of delivery of training and professional development is through workshops. Workshops are arranged in and by each IB region, details of which are available on the IB website. (Some subject workshops are now also available online.) As the name suggests, workshops are participatory in nature, and recognize the wealth of experience that practitioners bring to a workshop, which can be shared for the benefit of all participants. This is true of IB workshops for librarians, the approach to which varies in regions in the world, though the workshops are IBDP specific in the IBA and IBEAM regions.

In the Asia-Pacific region, a continuum approach is now offered; this is where one workshop is provided for librarians of the three programs, in which the continuum of key aspects is an important feature. Although librarians may break out into their relevant programs, in practice, librarians have found it valuable to be with librarians from other programs. For example, all three programs have a "concluding project"—the exhibition (PYP), personal project (MYP), and extended essay (IBDP), so there are common issues and opportunities for librarians of all programs, such as identifying a continuum of referencing skills. For the Asia-Pacific region, workshop leaders have developed a wiki that contains valuable and helpful practitioner-led information and knowledge products (see http://librarianscontinuum.wikispaces.com/).

The OCC is the main IB method of everyday information and support, and there are two moderators for the librarians' forum on the OCC. One focuses on the PYP, and the other on the MYP and the IBDP. The moderators are practicing librarians who undertake to regularly view posts that appear on different topics or threads, and provide some input or encourage other contributions from IB librarians around the world. The OCC has suffered an image problem in the past that is nothing to do with the excellent content and discussion it offers. It is worth persevering with it as it potentially offers a unique perspective to IB library issues (i.e., a world one), as the OCC is available and used worldwide. Other listservs and other self-help webgroups can of course offer excellent information, resources, and advice, but they may well be focused on the needs of a particular part of the world or a particular school type. In addition, the IB is looking at and developing its ICT, so it is recommended that librarians look—and contribute—regularly on the OCC. Part of the IB's ICT strategy is a new means of electronic communication for all IB stakeholders, called the IB Virtual Community (IBVC), launched in August 2010.

As well as the OCC, there may be subregional groupings (e.g., IB Mid-Atlantic) or more local ones, perhaps relating to an IB association, which tends to be national (e.g., the IB Association of Japan and Korea). Such groups may organize meetings and/or online means of communication. There are also voluntary library groups, often supported or encouraged by the IB regional offices, such as IBAP-LIS, which was instrumental in setting up the continuum workshop model in the IBAP region, and also encourages local communication between IB school librarians through its committee, which includes a representative from a number of the countries in the IBAP region.

As a curriculum, the IBDP developed initially with the involvement of teachers in international schools, and now from all types of schools that offer IB programs; teachers are also examiners (of which, there are over 6,000). Thus the curriculum has been and is significantly developed by practitioners. There is a policy that each IBDP subject's syllabus is revised every seven years, again with practitioner involvement, and this is also true of the extended essay and TOK requirements. Therefore, it is imperative that librarians are aware of the current requirements, which are all available on the OCC, usually in more than one language, in line with the IB's policy.

Furthermore, the IBDP coordinator receives a regular (usually quarterly) update from the IB called *Coordinator's Notes*, which notifies a school about recent changes and new developments (e.g., new set texts). Coordinators generally provide the link for the latest newsletter or host it on a school intranet, alerting faculty to its posting each time. Generally, the IBDP coordinator is a key figure in obtaining and distributing information from the IB and it is important that the librarian is in regular contact and liaison with the IBDP coordinator (Clark, 2006; Markuson, 1999).

For more detailed information about the IBDP, there are two books that a librarian, certainly one in a school new to the IBDP, may wish to read or have in a library professional collection to support the professional needs of faculty. These books are: Pound (2006) *The International Baccalaureate Diploma Programme: An Introduction for Teachers and Managers* and van Loo and Morley (2004) *Implementing the IB Diploma Programme: A Practical Manual for Principals, IB Coordinators, Heads of Department and Teachers*. Both books are edited texts, with contributions written by IBDP practitioners, thus they provide a wealth of experience, detail, and practical strategies on many aspects of the IBDP, though neither deals specifically with the role of the school library.

Current general information about the IB is published in its house magazine *IB World*, which is aimed at students, teachers, and parents; is published three times a year; and is also available online at the IB public website. A copy of the magazine should be made available in the school library. There is also the *IB World Schools Yearbook*, which includes profiles of schools that offer IB programs around the world.

PRACTICAL STRATEGIES FOR LIBRARIANS

- Librarians should be familiar with the latest IB *Programme Standards and Practices* and the *Guide to Programme Evaluation*.
- Librarians new to the IBDP should refer to the *Diploma Programme Guide* (2002) for a comprehensive yet brief overview. The latest version is always available on the OCC.
- Be aware of important documents issued by the IB (e.g., on internationalism and language development).
- Some IB documents contain helpful bibliographies or lists for further reading, and it may be beneficial if the librarian obtains a selection of these and other materials for a professional collection for teachers, both to assist with implementing the IBDP and as ongoing support for teachers in the program.
- Read the IB Mission Statement, and action it by relating it to library policies and documentation. Display the statement in the library.
- For librarians who know little about the program, say, in a candidate school, it may be helpful to read the IB document *Towards a Continuum of International Education*, to gain a pithy overview.
- Read John Royce's article *Walking Two Moons: Crossing Borders with International Literature* in Knowledge Quest (http://aasl.metapress.com/content/l31g520526276034/) to assist in an understanding of how internationalism may be reflected in the library collection.
- Ensure that internationalism or international mindedness is reflected in a library collection policy and ongoing practice.
- Review existing mother tongue collections in the library or consider starting relevant sections.
- Initiate discussion and ask for current international suggestions on a listserv, Google or Yahoo group, or similar local/regional network of school librarians (the group doesn't have to be specifically focused on the IB).
- Check the IB's OCC for ideas (http://occ.ibo.org/ibis/occ/guest/home.cfm).
- Check http://www.worldcat.org for relevant suggestions.
- Check the IB Librarians Continuum wiki for suggestions (https://librarianscontinuum.wikispaces.com/).
- Inquire about regional and/or local groups of IB librarians in your area. If there isn't an active group, think about starting an informal one for sharing information, perhaps as a one-off meeting, if distances between other IB schools make such an event feasible.
- Check the IB website for workshops for librarians in your IB region.
- Be aware of how the IB as an organization is constituted, evolving, and changing.
- Develop ongoing liaison with the IBDP coordinator. Obtain an e-copy of the regularly issued *Coordinator Notes*. Obtain hard copy of each issue of *IB World* for the library—several copies should be regularly mailed to the coordinator.
- Be aware of the authorization process in your region, if your school is at that stage, or the re-authorization procedure, and any requirements or involvement that could usefully involve the library and attendant deadlines.

- If you are concerned or wish to evaluate your library program's relevance to the IBDP, it may be helpful to follow the IB self-study process, purely as far as the school library is concerned. Even if your school is not yet due to undertake the authorization (or re-authorization) process, the self-study process is useful for your own management information purposes.

3

—•◆•—

THE IBDP SUBJECT MATRIX
AND CORE FEATURES

To complete the IBDP, candidates need to take classes in six subjects. They are also required to complete core requirements, so they follow a course in TOK, complete a CAS requirement, and research and write an individual extended essay. Students receive grades or marks, on a scale from 1 to 7, on successfully completing subject requirements. Subject requirements generally consist of assessed coursework and formal examinations. Assessed coursework may sometimes be referred to as "internal assessments" as they are initially marked by teachers at the school although they may also be moderated by teachers/examiners elsewhere. Formal examinations are externally set by the IB and marked, possibly by an examiner in another continent or IB region, at the end of the two-year program. For CAS, there is no mark or grade, but students are required to successfully complete CAS requirements. They are also awarded marks on an A–E and N (no grade) scale for completing their individual extended essay and an essay and presentation for TOK. Students need a total of 24 marks in order to gain the diploma, and marks rise to a maximum of 45, though the average mark is around 30. The mark structure is explained in various IB documents, but useful detail is to be found in *IB and Higher Education: Developing Policy for the IB Diploma Program Examinations* (International Baccalaureate Organization, 2009).

SUBJECT MATRIX

Students select a subject from a matrix of subject groups, referred to as groups 1 to 6. They represent languages, social sciences, pure sciences, mathematics, and arts, though they have their own specific terminology:

Group 1: Language (also known as language A1)
Group 2: Second language (also sometimes called language B)
Group 3: Individuals and societies
Group 4: Experimental sciences

Group 5: Mathematics and computer science
Group 6: The arts

Within each of the six groups, there are several options. Students select one option from each group. The idea is that students study one option from each of the main areas of human knowledge and endeavor, thereby achieving breadth in their learning. Depth of learning is achieved because students are required to take classes in three of the subjects at a higher level (HL) and the remaining three at a standard level (SL). Differences between HL and SL include the amount of time commitment needed, number of written requirements, and subject-specific differences.

Each subject has specific content or a syllabus, and these are outlined in detail in subject documents on the OCC. In practice, some subjects will be more amenable to library support than others. Nevertheless, the need for library support in certain subjects will vary from school to school. Library usage is often determined by individual teachers' preferences and their own history of library support and involvement. Some more detail about the subject groups and possible library implications is given below:

Group 1

In this language A1 group, students study literature in a student's first language, together with selections from world literature. The A1 group has over 40 language options, a reflection of the fact that the IBDP is a global curriculum. Students who come from all over the world, with very different first languages, are IBDP candidates. In the language A1 group, students should develop a personal understanding, response, and appreciation of literature; respect for their literary heritage; and an international perspective. The work of the A1 group also naturally enhances students' written and oral skills.

Students' study of literatures may involve students using the library for literary criticisms of authors and set works, and background information about historical periods and geographical regions relating to set texts (Clark, 2006). Because there are many options for different texts to be studied, this can be a challenge to a library and librarian to provide high-quality supporting materials, which are best developed through ongoing liaison with A1 faculty members.

The world literature element enables students to realize that literatures operate in a "pan-cultural context" that can be used to understand their own culture (Andain, Rutherford, & Allen, 2006, p. 57). The implication is for the school library to provide historical and contemporary examples of such literature.

Because reading certain texts is an essential element of a course in this group, some teachers suggest or require that students "get into the habit" by reading, reflecting, and commenting on or responding to a piece of creative writing during the long holiday preceding the start of the school year in which they begin their IBDP course. Teachers may suggest specific texts or ask the librarian to do so, or work together to produce a list. One such list, which focuses on a sense of place as a theme for the list, is reproduced in Appendix 3. Where there are large numbers of IBDP students each year, it may be helpful to develop a number of lists, perhaps with different themes. Or be more general with recommendations, and create a list by genre or output of an individual author. The goal is for students to have initial successful experiences when looking for required material in the library.

A librarian, working at an international school in Beijing, China, provided strategies for collaboration, cooperation, and liaison between librarian and teacher that could support group 1 subjects. These strategies included using the syllabus information provided by the English department as a guide, so that the librarian could purchase new titles in various media and inform the teachers when these are available. Other suggested strategies included regular attendance at English departmental meetings, provision of regular updates of additions to the library collection, collaboration on an extended reading project for students about contemporary literary texts in the first year of an IBDP course, distribution of a booklist for a pre-course holiday reading project, joint presentations to students with a teacher with debates on interesting reading material, and provision of training to students on research methods (Scribner, 2000).

Group 2

In this second language group, students study another language so that they can gain understanding of another culture and, naturally, acquire language proficiency. A variety of modern languages are possible, together with two classical languages, Latin and Greek; the exact language courses to be offered will inevitably vary from school to school. There are several options for learners at different levels in group 2. The range includes courses for students who have no knowledge of a particular language to those who are already proficient in a language, perhaps even to the extent of being bi- or trilingual and who study both culture and language. The terms used are, in order of ascending ability, *language ab initio*, *language B*, and *Language A2*. For these courses, there is a practitioner recommendation for resources that include "young adult fiction . . . [that] reflects contemporary issues in the target culture . . . written in a style that is linguistically rich and yet accessible" (Morley, 2004, p. 295). Some librarians have found that provision of various language magazines and databases, together with language collections in the library, have been helpful support for students in this group.

Group 3

Individuals and societies is a large subject group that features business and management; economics; geography; history; information technology in a global society; philosophy; psychology; social and cultural anthropology; and, since 2011, world religions. Whatever subject course students opt for, they should be able to critically analyze theory and ideas that relate to people, both as individuals and as members of a society.

For history, regular essay writing is required and an internal assessment is a considerable assignment of historical investigation for students; this internal assessment could involve cooperation or collaboration between history teacher and librarian resulting in booking library facilities, provision of training for students on databases, and more general guidance about researching and referencing, perhaps developed in a booklet or web-based text. Latuputty (2005) found that students at her school library tended to borrow audiovisual items related to history topics either for use in the library or at home. Occasionally, IB history essays are published in the *Concord Review*, and some of these previous issues are available on line, so librarians can see the standard that is required. Several commentators have recommended that students visit a local university library to allow access to specialized sources and documents, especially for internal assessment purposes.

For geography, case studies may be used, not least in film or DVD format. Note that feedback from IB workshops suggests that examples should not be more than five years old. This may be a factor for collection management policies and practices, where these items are part of the library collection (and developed in cooperation with geography faculty members).

Information technology in a global society (usually known as ITGS) looks at the effect of ICT on society in general, so research on this subject should use current information resources. As may be expected, given the pace of change of technology, the exact content of this course will change regularly. In the past, there have been annual themes, taking a particular form or use of technology, such as mobile phones. The course also looks at how technology affects people and organizations. The school library and librarian can be used as a case study, as in one school where the school librarian talked to students about how technology has changed libraries and librarians (specifically how they have reacted and responded to such changes), as well as the needs and perceptions of users. Such an opportunity can also provide a good way of demonstrating how the computer catalog and databases work. The librarian could promote a role for the library beyond the "printed page" or the physical library, but also in terms of providing electronic or digitized access to information, the librarian can demonstrate how the school library can be as an e-portal to information beyond the physical school location. Indeed, some teachers (Mueller & Stefanics, 2004) recommend that (a) "teachers should train students to cite references properly" to avoid plagiarism, using for instance Turnitin.com; (b) relevant skills include the ability to "manipulate databases," including the "school's electronic card catalog system"; and (c) the school library should provide books on computer ethics (p. 330).

Group 4

This experimental sciences group includes options in biology, chemistry, design technology, physics, and environmental systems. Again, whatever subject course students choose, the aim is that they analyze, evaluate, and use scientific theory and concepts. A common, compulsory element is that students need to look at social, ethical, and environmental implications of scientific advancement; this project can be collaborative and could be used to look at global issues.

With this group, the way of working is very practical. One librarian indicated that as the "sciences are very much lab-based, there has not been the need for extensive use of research materials," therefore alternative science textbooks could be provided as a discrete library collection to support students in this group, as is the case at an American international school in Hungary (Clark, 2006, p. 41). Some teachers encourage their students to read current general scientific periodicals, of which the best known are of course *Scientific American* and the *New Scientist*, both in hard copy and online, or available through databases. Teachers may suggest journals that are dedicated to specific subjects, for instance a particular science. There is some indication (Jones, 2004a) that the IB expects a library to provide various periodicals as well as other resources to support the IBDP in a particular school.

Group 5

This group comprises four mathematics courses of varying levels, of which the most general is called "mathematical studies standard level." An option to study computer science is available; where this is chosen, it is a requirement that a mathematics subject is also studied.

Although there is an international dimension to this group (students should understand the development of math through a variety of cultural perspectives and develop logical, critical thinking), again, this is a very practical subject group. It has been difficult to find references for possible library use for this group, though one source indicated that the computer science course "lends itself well to research on the Internet" (Dunkley, Banham, & Mcfarlane, 2006, p. 121), and Internet research can include using subscription databases.

Group 6

This group comprises film, music, theater, and visual arts, together with a new subject, dance (introduced in 2011). However, it is possible for a student to take a second subject from groups 1–5 instead of a group 6 subject.

Aims of courses in this arts group are to develop students' creativity and skills in critical reflection and practical research. Taking a group 6 subject will involve performance, practical project, or an exhibition of work. Likewise, group 6 subjects could also benefit from use of the library (e.g., works of drama production, dramatic and performance theory, etc.), and schools of art, such as using individual artists work as stimulus material. In one school, film classes were regularly held in a library room, as viewing a variety of movies by genre and referring to printed information and criticism about film genres were regular class and assignment activities. The film teacher cooperated with the librarian in developing a balanced collection of film genres (which was also available on loan to the wider school community). A feature of film and theater courses has been a requirement to make a critical response to specific plays and movies, and there may be a need to swiftly obtain such titles (which generally change each year). Required film titles have in the past been selected by genre or director, whereas the drama texts are taken from various historical periods and different parts of the world. For the music course, there is a requirement to study in depth one or more musical compositions; recent "set" works have ranged from an early opera by Purcell, a Mozart concerto, and Debussy's *La Mer*, to orchestral music by Aaron Copeland and David Fanshawe's *African Sanctus*. These titles indicate the specific level at which students are required to work. For such musical compositions, students benefit from listening to various recordings, which could be housed in a library audio collection or on-line service, and critical texts, which may be more associated with tertiary education level resources, but which may also be included, for instance, in an excellent music guide/companion series from Cambridge University Press. Recommended and set film, music, and theater titles are usually communicated to schools through the IBDP *Coordinator's Notes*.

Art students need to maintain a research workbook to show the development and influences on their work during their course. Students may be advised to show these workbooks at their exhibition of work (which is externally assessed) at the end of their course. It would be beneficial for a librarian to visit such exhibitions and look at the workbooks and talk to the students about their work. Talking with the students about their work could help provide ideas on how the library could support future IBDP art students. The library could be used to display various work in the facility. For example, one student's artistic response to a John Donne poem, seen by the school librarian at the annual IBDP art exhibition, was subsequently donated to the school library by the artist, where it was hung adjacent to the literature collection. As an example of the sort of research and inquiry involved, the following information written by a student was seen attached to a display of IBDP art in the public areas of one school: "[Title of artwork, artist/student name]. I've searched through the library to find sources that could show me how the body of a monkey could be sketched . . . most of my research came from the library, magazines, and the Internet. During this process, I found an artist called James Reekie, [also] Decamps and Tenners, but I was most influenced by Lassetter's photo collage of Bob Dylan."

In addition to the usual structure of the six subject groups, there may be some variations, including transdisciplinary subjects (such as environmental systems). The variations will depend on school circumstances, so the librarian should liaise with the school's IBDP coordinator to ascertain what exactly is being offered to students.

In the present writer's study, several teachers noted the lack of reference in IBDP subject documentation to using the school library and the librarians as a strategy in their pedagogical practice. Teachers were very specific about subject documentation, because this is where most teachers would tend to look for information. This lack of reference to school libraries in IBDP subject literature may contribute to a lack of a defined role and variable use, which in practice is reliant on individual teachers' interest and enthusiasm. In the discussion of the group subjects immediately above, with the exception of the librarian citation, there were only two brief mentions of library involvement in the IBDP teacher practitioner literature, even though resources and skills were commonly mentioned in these sources. This shows the possibilities and the need for librarians and teachers to report collaboration.

One significant comment by an IBDP practitioner does look at the role of the librarian in the IBDP. Jones (2004a) considered that the librarian should be involved in purchasing decisions related to "all reference materials for the school, including those materials that departments wish to order for themselves." Particular types of resources that should be provided include print and online encyclopedias, other subscription databases, antiplagiarism software services, periodicals (both print and online), English and foreign language newspapers and magazines, foreign language materials, various reference books, specific resources for TOK, and textbooks for subject areas. He dealt with the issue of centralizing resources and acknowledged that departments would maintain particular collections (which should nevertheless be centrally catalogued by the library staff). Furthermore, "departments should know what resources are available for their subjects in the library, and should work with the librarian to recommend reference texts. The same goes for TOK teachers" (p. 63).

When students are not in classes, they are allocated individual study times or "study halls," the freedom of which may be a new experience for a number of students. They may not have experienced this phenomenon before, which for a number of students is commonly called "free time"; but it may be that the most direct contact that librarians have with students in some schools could be during these times, especially if students are required to spend study time in the school library. (We will be returning to this aspect later in the book.)

It also may be worth thinking beyond a library role directly with students. The library's role can be developed through teachers, especially perhaps where smaller departments do not have departmental resources, but there are resources available in the library for both teachers and students. Again, it all depends on a teacher's preference, so response will be varied. Nevertheless, it is worthwhile for a librarian make subject links where possible. Much attention is rightly given to the extended essay as a main area for library support (discussed in the next chapter), but library support for the subject groups and TOK should be explored.

THEORY OF KNOWLEDGE (TOK)

Students are required to take a course in TOK, at the conclusion of which they complete an essay and make a presentation on a TOK theme. To gain a diploma, students are required to complete these assignments, and marks awarded for TOK requirements count towards their final overall mark. The marking structure is explained in the *Theory of Knowledge Guide for First Examinations 2008*, which is available on the OCC.

TOK is not, or should not, be seen as a course in philosophy, though it will use philosophical ideas and approaches. It is really a course in getting students to think widely and critically about their world and to challenge assumptions of knowledge and what they have hitherto thought of as knowledge. Basically, the course is designed to teach students to think "outside the box," to use an often-used term by IB practitioners. The TOK component was "designed to develop students' metacognitive skills and to challenge them to explore the bases of thinking and knowing" (Carber & Reis, 2004, p. 340). Indeed, "the strength of TOK is its commitment to inquiry," in the words of an IBO manager for TOK (Clarke, 2002, p. 11). One curriculum organization considered that TOK offered students "knowledge and experience gained inside and outside the classroom" and that students should be aware of bias and be able to analyze evidence rationally (Qualifications & Curriculum Authority, 2003, p. 1).

A central or desired element of TOK is critical thinking, on which librarians should focus their contribution. Rather than content per se, though also helpful as a focus, critical thinking is key to TOK work. Indeed, the "subject outline" for TOK can be pithily and graphically seen in "the TOK circle" or similar design. Whereas there is subject detail provided by the IB, TOK teachers and students often refer to the "TOK circle," which contains three rings within each other, showing concepts and their interrelationship to each other. These diagrams are *not* reproduced here as it would be helpful for an IBDP librarian to refer to the guide on the OCC, which includes these diagrams. While reading this guide, it might be helpful to bear in mind the following key terms (again, there is a specific IB/TOK language or jargon):

- Ways of knowing
- Areas of knowledge
- Truth
- Issues (formerly termed *problems*) of knowledge
- Authority

- Paradigm
- Knower(s)
- Language
- Belief
- Reason
- Sense perception

Each student's presentation may be presented individually or in small groups, but marks are awarded for each student. These can be on any topic, ranging from, for example, animal rights to parkour (which is sometimes called *freerunning*), where a person runs and does athletic movements in an urban environment. The topic that students choose are really a vehicle for exploring TOK concepts and ideas rather than a presentation of facts and their opinions on a particular issue, so a TOK presentation should be focused on how we know, what we know, and any problems or issues about knowing, as related to a particular issue.

Each student also needs to write a formal essay on 1 of 10 given titles, which change each year. The essay may involve research, in which case referencing is obviously required. Alternatively, students can prepare an essay that does not require formal research as the essay is really concerned with their balanced, critical viewpoints, based on TOK principles. Marks are awarded for essay structure and ideas, personal and other examples, relationship to key TOK concepts, and referencing (if a student has used sources). Examples of essay titles from previous years (which are available on the OCC) indicate the degree of inquiry and critical thinking required by students:

- Discuss the roles of language and reason in history.
- "There are no absolute distinctions between what is true and what is false." Discuss this claim.
- To what extent do we need evidence to support our belief in different areas of knowledge?
- How important are the opinions of experts in the search for knowledge?

TOK could be a major focus of support for the school library. In IB library workshops that I have led, one activity centered on library support for TOK. Participants were asked to add a fourth circle to the "TOK circle," adding library support they thought would be helpful or perhaps had used in their own schools. The following are some examples of ideas generated by participants:

- Collaborate with TOK teachers. Collaboration with supervisors, teachers, and students.
- Develop collection, including books, journals, online databases, audio visual materials, and newspapers. Resource creative texts, film, multimedia, databases, and magazines, including *Philosophy Now, New Scientist, Smithsonian,* and so forth. Include primary and secondary sources. Develop a balanced collection that demonstrates opposing viewpoints.
- Represent a variety of cultural viewpoints in library collection. Find material to provide stimulus to students.

- Develop mother tongue collections, including foreign language texts and newspapers.
- Provide a dedicated TOK "core" collection.
- Provide essay examples and resource guides for essay titles.
- Develop knowledge of "expert" people to come and speak. Identify links to wider community. Create lists of personal contacts.
- Promote intercultural communication.
- Promote the concept of Dewey classifications 000–999 = areas of knowledge.
- Provide suitable environment for this learning by developing collaborative flexible work spaces in the library. Provide flexibility of library by extending hours.
- Host a lunch-time "soap box." Create soap box graffiti board.
- Create engaging displays (e.g., of banned books or TOK themes).
- Manage virtual classroom space.
- Show students how to use equipment (i.e., for presentations).
- Support research-based essays or presentations, via information online, texts, or referencing assistance.
- Foster questioning skills, debate (e.g. bookclubs, blogs).
- Provide teaching of advanced research skills. Assist in identifying search terms and unpacking questions. Develop critical and creative thinking skills using collection, activities, lessons, explicit keys like thinking hats and Art Costa's work.
- Teach how to use graphic organizers; how to study/how to compile bibliography booklets.
- Teach research and information literacy skills, research process (scaffolding/support), bibliographic skills. Give explicit instruction in referencing skills.
- Provide individual student counseling. Be a mentor. Assist in formulating and unpacking questions. Act as sounding board for students.
- Develop understanding of the Dewey Decimal Classification System of organizing knowledge.
- Contribute an organization of knowledge class.
- Model understanding and acceptance of different viewpoints.
- Demonstrate knowledge management skills.
- Model and promote academic honesty.

These suggestions have been grouped into four discrete areas that are familiar to job activities that are associated with librarians and reflect trends in the literature about school librarianship. These areas are:

- Collaboration
- Resource and information provision and expertise
- Management of a facility
- Teaching and tutoring

Some of these suggestions are more general (and so could be related to TOK as any other curriculum area), while other suggestions are specific tasks focused on the TOK syllabus. It would be worth exploring any of these suggestions in support of a TOK program.

Another role is possible, that of a regular TOK teacher. Teachers of TOK do not come from one discipline, nor should they. Faculty members teach TOK because they are interested in working with students in a constructivist manner. Ideally TOK faculty represent all or at least a majority of different areas of school life. It is possible for a librarian to become involved with teaching TOK, either on an ad hoc basis or as a regular member of the TOK team. There are TOK training workshops held by the IB and, just like other subject and library workshops, attending these is a requirement for those teaching IB programs. It is also possible to become a TOK examiner for the IB, but a person needs to be a TOK teacher to qualify as an examiner. The e-mail that is reproduced below is one I sent in reply to a librarian, who asked on a listserv about how to become a TOK teacher, either on an occasional basis or full time. It may give an idea of some of the issues involved:

I really started as a TOK teacher by providing a one-off session about how knowledge is/could be organized (and which really related to the Dewey Decimal Classification System). The session actually came about after a casual conversation about TOK with one of the teachers. However, within weeks, I became a regular TOK team-teacher, as a school's TOK teaching team may well welcome new ideas—and faces.

If you want some ideas about how you could be involved in the TOK teaching program to present to your IBDP coordinator, I hope the following will be of interest. When students are looking at what a knower/knowledge is, you could offer a session on how knowledge is arranged/organized, etc., that would fit well, perhaps bringing in the idea of "authority" in knowledge (e.g., the academic paper system) and problems (or "issues" as the current TOK terminology has it) of knowledge, and differentiating between knowledge and information, etc.

If your school organizes the outline of the TOK course around the circle, it might be good to have a few sessions so you're involved in each circle, therefore students are reminded of your role as an occasional TOK teacher throughout their course—I agree with you, getting senior students (including perhaps students who are not library users) to see you as an IBDP teacher is a good move.

In terms of the Ways of Knowing, why not teach something about language—perhaps looking at jargon, for instance, how this limits "knowledge" to an in-crowd or elite who understand the jargon/acronyms particular to a certain group; also academic language versus texting or similar; subject terms vs. natural language.

In the Areas of Knowledge, as part of Ethics, why not teach something about plagiarism/academic honesty?

At my school, we used lots of current news pieces, short exercises, and lots of table discussions, which suited our students, especially EAL [English as a second language], mixed ability ones—as all students in grades 11–12 did IBDP. We didn't issue textbooks to students, but we had some copies in the library for ideas, stimulus material. We found a TOK book by Richard van de Lagemaat especially helpful.

Another way we did it was for each teacher to take a way of Knowing and/or an Area of Knowledge and offer a module on that, so students moved around that, so thinking of how you could do one of those might be helpful, and at the same time limit involvement, so that it doesn't take too much time.

A TOK COLLECTION IN THE LIBRARY

The library should provide support for TOK in terms of developing relevant library resources, whether books, DVDs, databases, periodicals, or newspapers. Liaise or collaborate with TOK teachers in such a development. This collection could be wide-ranging in subject (or at least Dewey Decimal Classification System) coverage. A wide-ranging collection of titles can create problems, as relevant items would naturally be disbursed throughout the collection. One possible advantage is that teachers and students may find other helpful resources while looking for specific items, but the corresponding disadvantage could be that they might not bother to look. Ways around this include tagging relevant TOK resources in the computer catalog, such as a resource list, or using "Theory of Knowledge" as a subject term.

Another option is to provide a discrete collection in the library. This could bring together various media, and still preserve a classification. Prefix the classification number with "TOK" and house it in a specific area, advertised by clear guiding, such as "TOK Collection." While this could limit where students (and teachers) look, it may be helpful to users to have just one place to look for sources. If, however, you decide to make this a core collection, you could indicate that there are other helpful resources in the main library collection, and perhaps use one of the methods identified in the previous paragraph to help locate these.

What to include in such a collection? Look for items that explore the concepts identified in the TOK guide on the OCC, plus themes TOK teachers want to explore, along with other stimulating material. Relevant items are suggested in Appendix 1, and other ideas could come from looking at the librarian's forum on the OCC and asking for current ideas and titles; gathering suggestions from IB library workshops; or looking on the Internet to see if other schools have their TOK resources listed online. It is likely that a number of titles will be academic in nature, given the abstract nature of the concepts and ideas concerned; however, it is important to provide more readable, brief, and "quirky" items (such as graphic nonfiction).

Although books may be the dominant medium, it is helpful to remind teachers and students that databases, periodicals, and newspapers can contain helpful information. These sources could also be used by teachers, especially if they are looking for topical items to illustrate a given topic and to stimulate discussion around a particular theme. This is particularly so where differentiated topic group or table discussion and feedback techniques, Socratic dialogue, or other generally constructivist approaches to learning are used for TOK classes. One teacher advocated a seminar approach to teaching classes aided by "books . . . articles from newspapers and periodicals, and videos [that] can all provide a valuable stimulus for discussion and analysis" (Austin, 2006, p. 40). In some schools, students are asked to collect materials from newspapers and magazines (whether online or in hard copy) that illustrate TOK themes. Information items may also be used by students to suggest an idea or theme for their assessed TOK presentation and as concrete examples (which are required) for their TOK essay. Some teachers use movies to support themes as students can empathize with the characters and situations. Again, these could be made available in the library.

While a TOK collection is largely reliant on the librarian's skills, organization, and knowledge in its development, it is also worth promoting the role of the librarian as a source of information or a knowledge management role. This includes providing information about sources outside school, people and organizations, such as charities, local voluntary groups, district, city and government agencies, and higher education.

The extended essay is the focus of the next chapter. A link between the work done for the TOK and the extended essay may be seen in that TOK challenges students to think creatively, critically, and widely, and the extended essay is an opportunity for students to show that they can apply such skills. The other remaining element of the IBDP core is CAS [community, action, and service]. As its title suggests, this element requires students to be involved in service and action in the community, however that community is defined. It could be local, regional, or global. For instance, there may be more opportunities for involvement in a larger, urban environment. Also, in an international school context, there may be local, legal issues that affect how or if students volunteer in the community. It depends on the context of the school. Again, there is a guide to CAS requirements on the OCC; there should also be a CAS coordinator in your school to supervise each IBDP student as they all need to complete CAS requirements. The library may have a role in providing information about possible projects and local community information that will help students identify projects that they can be involved in.

PRACTICAL STRATEGIES FOR THE LIBRARIAN

- Become familiar with IBDP terminology as it relates to subject areas and core requirements.

- Look at the subject documents on the OCC prior to talking to subject faculty members about library support for individual subjects within the IBDP subject matrix.

- Accept that a library response to groups and individual subjects within groups will inevitably vary with the subject and a teacher's preferred way of working.

- Talk to the CAS coordinator about ways in which the library can support CAS needs of students.

- Think about becoming involved in the TOK course as a resource provider, librarian, TOK teacher, or all three.

- Consider how the library can best provide relevant information resources and support for the convenience of TOK students and teachers.

- Prior to considering how to support your students in their library usage, check out unofficial websites (e.g., www.ibtokspot.blogspot.com) to see what students think and what their concerns are.

4

THE EXTENDED ESSAY

The extended essay is a unique feature of the IBDP in which each IBDP candidate is required to complete an individual research essay or paper. This is a formal piece of work, involving a "proper abstract, a complete bibliography and a closely-argued text, and adequately supported by data" (Austin, 2006, p. 160). Schools can set various internal deadlines for the stages and completion of the extended essay, but all students are required to plan, research, and write a formal essay of no more than 4,000 words. Each essay receives a grade that contributes towards an individual student's final mark. Each student, who has to successfully complete an extended essay in order to be awarded a diploma, has a supervisor for the essay who is usually a member of the school staff. The IBDP coordinator usually has overall charge of the extended essay, though in larger cohorts of IBDP students, an extended essay coordinator may be appointed (which may be the librarian). An IB guide to the extended essay is available on the OCC, and the librarian should be familiar with the latest version, which was issued in December 2010. This document contains regulations that students have to follow.

The value of the extended essay has been identified by a number of individuals and organizations, including the UK's Qualification and Curriculum Authority (2003), which has said that the essay "acquaints candidates with the kind of independent research and writing skills expected by universities" (p. 1). The core of the IBDP was also regarded as providing effective preparation for life in tertiary education by staff in Australian and New Zealand universities, and in research undertaken by the Australian Council for Educational Research (Coates, Rosicka, & MacMahon-Ball, 2007). In an article concerning research about the extended essay, Munro (2003) found that by undertaking an extended essay students could go further than understanding existing knowledge; they could make their own knowledge. He found that students needed motivation and self-management for independent learning, time management (the essay is an extended piece of work that may take a student 40 hours to complete, which is the IB's general guideline), creative thinking, and developing information literacy to select, organize, and evaluate information before offering a new hypothesis.

This writer's study found that the extended essay is often perceived to be the main focus of library support. The essay process prepares students for the type of independent research and writing expected in higher education; in this, citation and referencing skills are very important, yet in the IBDP literature, there are only isolated references to the role of librarians in this regard (such as Jones, 2004b).

Student experiences are varied, not least regarding use of resources in libraries. For instance, Voipio (1993) found there were no relevant resources to support his topic. He genuinely developed new knowledge and subsequently applied for a patent for his invention. Another student used the library infrastructure of the country she was in, but found limited items (Yip, 2000). Both these students' experiences may be far from unusual, as students are expected to provide original insights or look at a problem that few may have looked at before. Therefore, finding little in the way of relevant resources is an issue (Petersen, 2003) but should not necessarily be seen as a negative aspect though someone may need to point this out to students. However, students do need to base their essay hypothesis on research if at all possible, and they may not perceive that they need to conduct a general to specific literature search, nor will they typically have experiences about looking widely in the literature. Alternatively, some students tend to write their essays in areas that have received a lot of coverage over the years (in terms of extended essays), such as specific wars, dictators, and variations on themes of previous essays in that school. Equally, some students have developed "serious pieces of local history . . . and some high quality scientific reports based on individual fieldwork and experiments" (Mathews & Hill, 2005, p. 162). But students do need adult help and support, though the essay must be initiated, driven, conducted, and completed by students.

Jones (2004b) recommends that the IBDP coordinator should maintain oversight of the essay process, but "work in tandem with the teacher-librarian." If students discuss ideas early enough, the librarian could obtain specific material for the student. A workshop on researching could be held that would enable students to maximize and benefit from using the library. It is important to make "firm and explicit links between the library, faculty and students; otherwise many students will never use the school library for their extended essay." A librarian has a role in advising both teachers (i.e., essay supervisors) and students about "research, referencing and essay structure" (pp. 198–199). This is the most developed statement from a non-LIS source of the library's and librarian's involvement in the extended essay.

Given that a main function for a school librarian in the IBDP is to support the extended essay, it may therefore suggest a hidden role for libraries, as it is not identified in documents or research. Alternatively, students may make other arrangements, perhaps using departmental or teachers' personal libraries, or having access to university libraries. Alternative options for research will vary from school to school.

From the literature and the writer's study, it may be suggested that there are several issues for the school librarian to be aware of in relation to the extended essay:

- Librarians were typically not used enough.
- Librarians should be consulted early in the process, in order to provide the best-quality help.
- Librarians could even suggest against a topic, especially where little material exists, except where it is likely that a student could develop new knowledge or an invention or new product.

- Teachers may not be aware of the role of libraries. Where teachers are supervisors, their advice to students is crucial, and that advice may not include overtly recommending library use.

- Students may need to access a library and information infrastructure beyond their own school library.

- Students and/or teachers and librarians could make useful links with local universities.

- Librarians should provide a range of extended essays, as exemplars, in the school library collection.

- Website and online support could be developed, both for information and advice.

- School-based essay writing guides could be written by librarians.

- Librarians could provide support and tuition in terms of online databases, which students may have never used previously.

- An assessment could be made of students' research skills at this point of their IBDP candidature. Are their skills sufficient for the tasks ahead of them?

TITLES OF EXTENDED ESSAYS

After understanding the requirements of the extended essay, one of the first things that students do when beginning the extended essay process is to identify a topic that really interests them and then narrow this topic down to a question.

This section shows the specific and original nature of extended essays, including a review of extended essay titles details that are mentioned in the literature. Also included is an analysis of titles and the grades specific extended essays were awarded. It is considered good practice to provide helpful examples (Dando, 2004; Wallace, 2003) so that students can see the standard to be aimed for and what is involved. This section therefore shows the range of possible topics and questions. The choice of topic will depend partly on their skill in obtaining supporting material and a librarian's ability in resourcing very specific extended essay questions.

The specialized nature of an essay could be seen from the title of an essay completed by an international school student in the United States: *To What Extent Did the Alliance of Ibn Sa'ud and the Ikhwan During the 1920s Lead to the Achievement of their Respective Goals* (Elwan, 1989). This was included in a special IB issue (published in 1991) of *The Concord Review*, a quarterly journal that publishes outstanding essays written by mostly United Students high school students studying history. This specialized journal also publishes other essays, such as that by a student at an international school in Japan, which was entitled *Who Became Kamikaze Pilots, and How Did They Feel towards Their Suicide Mission?* (Sasaki, 1996). *The Concord Review* continues to publish IB essays (both extended essays and coursework essays in history) from time to time, some of which are available online.

IB World, the IB's house magazine, previously published essays to celebrate achievement and to provide exemplars. One such essay was *Spoken Canadian English: Regional Variations and National Characteristics* (Hardman, 1994). Excerpts from several essays, with comments from examiners were also published in the issue (issue 15, 1997). Dickinson (1997) commented of one that "the bibliography . . . and the thoroughness of the argument provide clear evidence of the extensive research and careful reflection underpinning this essay" (p. 27). Although the essay relied on two sources in particular, overall the standard of critical thinking and writing was judged excellent.

Some school websites may provide examples of essay titles. These three titles, completed in 2009, are taken from the website of the Cairo American College (2010) in Egypt: *How Can the International Continental Hotels Company Maximize Profits of their International Hurghada Resort?* (subject area: business and management); *The Success of Egyptian New Towns: A Case Study of Al Rehab City* (subject area: geography); *Muse and Abuse: An Analysis of the Misconception of Jihad and How It Led to the Current Political Situation* (subject area: peace and conflict studies).

Essays in experimental sciences provide students with an opportunity to undertake a significant investigation. Examples of topic areas and questions that students have chosen at one United Kingdom school include: behavior in woodlice; abiotic index, abiotic factors, and the water quality of the River Cam; comparison of methods to analyze the vitamin C content of fruit drinks (Dunkley, Banham, & Macfarlane, 2006).

The OCC included a list of essay titles from an international school at Vienna, in Austria. Held as a resource on the database, this was a response to an inquiry (in December 2005) on the IB librarians' forum (listserv) for examples of titles. Titles and relevant subject areas included:

> *Is KL [Kuala Lumpur] International Airport an Example of a Form Following Function or Function Following Form?* (Art and Design)
>
> *The Breeding Behaviour of Great Tits (Parus Major)* (Biology)
>
> *MacDonald's in Vienna: A Monopoly?* (Economics)
>
> *Living in a Virtual, 3D world?* (ITGS)
>
> *How Does the Increase of Reinforcement Material Affect the Strength of a Composite Material* (Physics)
>
> *Instrumental Music in the Sema Ritual (Mevlevi)* (Music)
>
> *Is Method Acting the Ultimate Technique for Actors or Can Other Contrasting Methods Be Used?* (Theatre Arts)

Specifically for language A1, successful examples of titles were:

> *An Exploration of Aristotle's Tragic Form in "Oedipus Rex" by Sophocles and "Death of a Salesman" by Arthur Miller*
>
> *The Metaphor of Music: The Use of Music to Express the Paradox of Love and War in the Text and Film Versions of "Captain Corelli's Mandolin."* (Morley, Beverley, & Ruhil, 2004, p. 246)

For group 4 subjects, Hunter, Payne, and Hobman (2004), who agreed with a general view that choice of title was essential for success, provided alternative title examples, such as *"How Effective Are Different Golf Ball Designs in Increasing Spin?* rather than *The Physics of Golf"*; *"The Effect of Banana Peel on Seed Germination* rather than *Factors that Affect the Germination of Seeds"*; *"Can Polarimetry Be Used to Analyse the Purity of Sugars?* rather than *Analysis of Fruit Juice"* (p. 405).

Retrieved from the library collection of an international school in Japan, the following titles are from extended essays, written between 2003 and 2005 that had been awarded grades A and B:

Water Pollution Management Techniques and their Impact on [names of rivers in a specific city]

  Subject: Geography   Grade: A

Why Doesn't the Japanese Horse Race World Breed Pure Domestic Blood Strain Horses? (Title translated from Japanese)

  Subject: Japanese   Grade: A

Did the USA Impose its Legal System on Japan? A Case Study of the Law of Child Custody

  Subject: History   Grade: B

In what Ways do Japanese Boys' Comics Show a Different Approach to Those of the USA?

  Subject: Visual Arts   Grade: B

To What Extent Was the Third Reich Influenced by Heinrich Himmler's Occult Ideas?

  Subject: History   Grade: B

To What Extent Was Mao, and Not Stalin, the Leader of the World Communist Movement from 1949 to 1953?

  Subject: History   Grade: B

The Reasons Why Mystery Stories Are Loved by Readers (translated from Japanese)

  Subject: Japanese   Grade: B

A Comparative Investigation, using Graph Theory, of the Efficiency of two Metropolitan Railway Systems (Comparing Sydney and Tokyo)

  Subject: Mathematics   Grade A

Wonderful Code Switching

  Subject: Japanese   Grade A

Was the Atomic Bomb Employed against Japan by the Americans in 1945 Justified?

  Subject: History   Grade A

A Comparative Study of Japanese and Chinese Textbooks and Their Depiction of Japanese Aggression in China 1895–1937

  Subject: History   Grade A

What Are the Historical Reasons for the Controversy that Surrounds the Yasukuni Shrine in Tokyo?

  Subject: History   Grade A

Why Is Genji Monogatari by Murasaki Shikibu Popular Now Amongst Mainly Women? (Title translated from Japanese)

  Subject: Japanese   Grade B

What Are the Factors Affecting the Flight of Ornithopters?

  Subject: Physics   Grade B

Aging Problem in Japan and Other Countries: A Comparison of Policy (translated from Japanese)

Subject: Japanese   Grade B

To What Extent Did the 2.26 Incident in 1936 Contribute to the Establishment of the Military Rule in Japan?

Subject: History   Grade B

What Is the Significance and Influence of Yohaku in Japanese Traditional Byobu Paintings?

Subject: Visual Arts   Grade B

What Is the Role of School at the Present Day? (translated from Japanese)

Subject: Japanese   Grade B

While there is far more to an essay than the title, the practice of refining a topic area to a specific title that will focus investigation and inquiry and is not merely description is something that many students find difficult, and support, whether from an essay supervisor or others, such as a librarian, can be helpful. The titles above are all different in terms of their composition: some are short and pithy whereas others have sub-clauses; some are direct questions whereas others are statements. All the essay titles, though, are very specific (both in subject and geographical terms), and often some of the essays break new ground in that there may be little information available on the subject being studied. On the other hand, there are a couple of topic areas above that contain possibly many resources (e.g., World War II), yet, by choosing a question that focuses on a particular or new angle, students can use and refer to some more general resources to support the original angle chosen. (Using general sources for specific information can be a subtle use of resources that students may not appreciate, so familiarizing students with the practice of extracting specific information from more general information sources may involve the librarian showing students particular chapters, sections, or pages in some resources as examples.)

Choosing a topic and refining a question is an individual response. For some students, they will thrive on the challenge of producing new knowledge or insight, while others need the support (but not the crutch) of resources to help them in their research and critical response to the question they have chosen.

The librarian can play an advisor role in drafting the question and, at the same time, give advice about possible resources or sources. In some schools, students meet with the librarian about their extended essay as an integral part of the internal process and doing so is included on a checklist that students have to follow. In other schools, the IBDP coordinator provides a list of the chosen essay questions to the librarian. In practice, exact procedures vary, perhaps according to the personalities involved, the size of the school, and its library (including staffing levels) and the local available infrastructure. In a presentation to students, the librarian can include or discuss the skills involved in developing tight, specific questions that allow an investigative approach.

PRESENTATION ABOUT THE LIBRARY'S ROLE

One experienced commentator (Jones, 2004b) suggested that giving a presentation to students about the library's role in the extended essay process is good practice, and, indeed, many librarians offer something in this line, preferably in conjunction with the IBDP coordinator, as the latter's "stamp of approval" and involvement in the presentation is important to students. On a very practical note, the coordinator will be aware of internal deadlines associated with the extended essay. To be most effective and helpful, follow "just-in-time" principles in presenting to students what they need to know at a particular moment.

What follows is one example of what to include in a presentation, class, or seminar about essay writing and the needs of the extended essay. It could be one course or a series of short presentations given over a period of time. For instance, in one school, three short presentations were made to grade 11 students (who attended on a voluntary basis, with a high rate of attendance) during their lunch break, and the presentations were given on an annual basis. (If some of the information and points that follows appears basic, it is best to cover all eventualities, especially if your school has a mobile or transient student population. Also, the points reflect some experiences of the present writer, who was for some years, an examiner for TOK essays.)

Students may be often told of the requirements of the extended essay, and will invariably look on it as a huge commitment, which it is, but the librarian needs to find a new angle to engage student attention. Students will probably not reflect on the importance of the process and the value of the experience to each student, especially for the future, such as when they are in higher education, as they are not used to the idea of deferred gratification. Therefore, to start with a benefit to students may be more effective than listing requirements and deadlines, which they may have heard before elsewhere. So, suggest to students that the process and experience of writing an extended essay will help them write any relevant essay they need to write in support of college applications. Students could also refer to the research process and skills they developed during their viva (a relatively new requirement of the extended essay), which is a meeting they hold with their supervisor after the extended essay has been completed. Therefore, highlight for students important aspects of the extended essay experience, such as

- Critical thinking
- Time management
- Value of the extended essay experience to individual students
- Value of research as a means to add to a student's thinking and supports his/her views

In a presentation, the librarian should also focus on how to cite and construct a bibliography. It is useful to explain that accurate and systematic citing shows academic honesty, and by providing good citations feeds back to a main element of IB's philosophy. Failure to do so amounts to plagiarism. To remove any impression among students that citation refers only to books, it is helpful to explain that research sources can include books, journal articles, newspaper reports, Internet sources, maps, films, illustrations, graphic images, and so on. It is useful also to introduce the terms (and distinguish between) intellectual copyright and creative commons, that is, to advise students that not everything they see on the Internet can be used freely and without attribution of the original creator(s).

Librarians can promote subscription databases, which for many students could well be a new way of accessing information. Students will need help with navigating databases (a need they may be unaware of having), so a demonstration could form part of a presentation. Students should understand that databases are different from information they may get on the free web, and these databases may feature whole-text articles and other sources. Databases may also provide features (such as helping them cite references accurately) that are not available on the Internet.

Also explain how educators view and regard information sources. This is an important distinction to make as it will usually be different from how students see information. It is important for students to appreciate that there is a more formal way of looking at reliable sources of information, as educators will be marking this academic, formal piece of work. For instance, one LIS study (Merchant & Hepworth, 2002) found that:

- "Print sources, with the exception of newspapers and magazines, were viewed as sources of information [by educators] with which to build a framework for the topic, the theory behind what was to be taught, or for factual information." (p. 83)
- "The internet in particular, and also TV, subject journals, newspapers and magazines were considered to provide current, supplementary information." (p. 83)

Assume that students have not used the library. Ask rhetorical questions, such as "did you look in the library?" "Did you consult the catalog, look around the shelves, or give up?" Make a distinction between the library and the librarian so as to promote the role of the librarian as a research skills tutor, one-on-one advisor, and specific support provider irrespective of what is in the library. This is realistic, given the very specific nature of extended essays, as identified above.

As mentioned above, focus on citation in text and bibliography construction, which again may be a new requirement or practice for some students. It is also a key area of expertise that is associated with librarians. Explain precisely the options:

- Numbering system or author, date (and page number if a quote)
- One bibliography listing (no separate notes listing necessary)

It will also be helpful to show students:

- What citation in text looks like on the printed or word-processed page
- How to handle quotations—include author, date and page number (e.g., "Taylor, 2005, p. 10")
- How to paraphrase text—cite author and date (e.g., "Taylor, 2005")
- The difference between paraphrasing, direct quotation, and acknowledging an idea, with clear examples

Also discuss some more basic ideas or reminders about bibliography, such as

- In a bibliography, items should be in the same order as cited in text (i.e., if students have cited "Wallace & Gromit, 2003" in the text, the bibliography entry should start with *W* and not *G* and not by the first letter of the first word of the title). Also, items should be compiled in one alphabetical listing, whatever the format of the source of information. Do not organize listings by format. (By indicating that this helps a reader to find sources easily also makes the point to students that bibliographies *are* helpful, practical documents, and not just an academic requirement that individuals are not likely to use. If students see the point of something, they are more likely to follow or do it.)

- Follow one system of citation for all sources of information used. In other words, students. should be consistent in their application of a particular system.

- Give students strategies about what to do when they think they cannot find bibliographic information, such as by going to the root of a URL to find the home page, which may contain authorial information.

- Challenge their concept of what an author is (i.e., organizations, such as a schools, nongovernmental organizations [NGOs], government departments, and commercial organizations can all be authors).

- Show basic errors that occur when citing websites (e.g., a URL alone is not a citation or a reference).

- Although students can use various (often free) bibliography-construction services on the Internet, it is still worthwhile to briefly explain the principles behind the system.

Librarians should model good practice, so, for instance, if a PowerPoint or handout is used, include citations in text and a bibliography at the end. This gives students concrete examples they can follow. Encourage teachers to do similarly.

Involve students from previous years in your seminar, if at all possible, whether in real life, on video, or through quotations, such as these comments from students who had completed the process:

> The examiners love to hear about different countries and cultural experiences. So if it is possible to relate it to one country, it would be beneficial. They also give higher marks to those with primary resources such as an interview with a war veteran, etc. . . . Try to relate a general topic to something that happened recently, e.g., SARS (for mathematics—the extended essay received an A grade).
>
> Choose your topic carefully; don't leave it to the last minute; record every source you find useful; read and re-read the guidelines.

If it is not possible to use student experiences in this way (perhaps because your school is new to the IBDP), then use a book written and published by a student, *Three: The Ultimate Student's Guide to Acing Your Extended Essay and Theory of Knowledge* (Zouev, 2008). Or use other published student experiences that have been published from time to time in the IB house magazine *IB World*.

Content of a presentation by a librarian could also include "tips" on how to formulate a question and write an essay title. Librarians could use previous years' examples (and give a grade for the essay), to stimulate students' thinking. Without mentioning the names of individual students, it is useful to give local examples, as these seem more real to students. A brief analysis of some titles has been indicated above, but tips could include:

- Essay titles should be very specific.

- Titles should be written so that they encourage an investigative approach, not a descriptive one.

- Students should write and re-write possible essay titles—this drafting process is important. Going with the first title a student thinks of could be a costly mistake.

- Can students memorize their chosen title? This strategy can help some students to clarify their question, as they will typically be spending a good deal of time on the essay and they want to be sure of the title. For other students though, they like to write it down in several places (e.g., on pin-boards in their bedrooms) so that they do not forget it, or go "off track."
- Remind students that the librarian is available for consultation on a one-to-one basis for discussion about an individual student's essay title (though students should also inform their supervisor about a librarian's help).

While a seminar about the research aspect of the extended essay should be timed just before a student starts the extended essay process, finding curriculum time may be an issue, and scheduling should be discussed with the IBDP coordinator well ahead of time. If and when library support is seen as valuable and helpful, it could be readily added to the annual cycle in a timetable. (Though not recommended, it appears that some librarians have been able or encouraged to use TOK timetabled sessions for their extended essay presentations.)

THE ABSTRACT

A school librarian may also be involved in another aspect of the process that may be new for students—the abstract, which is required from each student. Writing an abstract comes at the end of the extended essay process and may be overlooked or left to individual supervisors to advise. There may be an assumption that students have this skill already. Indeed, students may have experience in stretching their writing to cover x number of words, but they don't necessarily have experience in writing concisely, with clear, unambiguous meaning, so may be a need to provide practice and advice in developing this skill.

The Essay Guide for examinations starting in 2013 indicates that a formal abstract needs to be provided in each student's extended essay. Students must take account of the following:

- Each abstract should not be longer than 300 words.
- The abstract should not be merely an introduction to the essay.
- The abstract should provide a summary of the whole essay and, to enable students to write a better abstract, it should be one of the last things a student does in the extended essay process.
- As a minimum, the abstract should indicate clearly the question that has been researched, how wide the inquiry was, and the conclusions.
- There are clear instructions about how the abstract should be presented and where it should appear in the extended essay.

As the extended essay document indicates, the abstract is included in the process because it requires students to analyze and articulate the development of their argument in the essay.

Students, supervisors, and librarians should consult the extended essay document for this requirement as with all other requirements. The document is available online on the OCC.

Here, a student may benefit from individual support from the librarian or provision of a written help-sheet, which can be posted online. An excellent example of an extended essay abstract in chemistry is reproduced in Dunkley, Banham, and Macfarlane's (2006) paper on mathematics and the sciences in Pound's (2006) *The International Baccalaureate Diploma Programme: An Introduction for Teachers and Managers*. The reproduced abstract or the extended essay entitled "Investigating chemiluminescence" is available on pages 143–144.

SUPPORTING STUDENTS IN THEIR EXTENDED ESSAY NEEDS

- The librarian should be involved in supporting individual students with resources, once students are nearer to deciding or have decided upon both their topics and questions. Obtain specific resources for students in the school library and, if appropriate, make arrangements to borrow specific items through an interlibrary loan service or other means in a regional library infrastructure. For example, in one school only one or two students undertook an essay in mathematics each year, but each required specific articles in mathematics journals that were not available in subscription databases. To find the required articles needed, the librarian used document supply services of various national libraries, such as the British Library and the National Library of Australia, as well as commercial services.

- In schools where extended essays may predominate in literature and social sciences, be aware that this could have an implication for school library collection development.

- Provide examples of previous extended essays that were completed at the school. A collection of completed essays can act as a bank of recommended examples for students to follow in terms of the format and the types of essay questions that may be more successful. It could be helpful to add a grade to these essays. A specific policy may be needed so that the library can keep essays that are recommended and manage this collection. An example of such a policy is provided at Appendix 6. (Some schools have a policy of asking students for a copy of their essay for the library.) Once a collection grows, it may be helpful to catalog and classify essays. The essays could be available either for reference in the library or loaned to students. Another option would be to digitize the contents; however, it is best to liaise with the IBDP coordinator about identifying legal ownership of each essay and determining whether digitization is helpful in a local school situation.

- In any extended essay section, think about including various published guides to writing essays; please see a list of some titles at Appendix 5. Some of these titles were suggested in various contributions to a question about recommended resources for essay writing on a listserv for international school librarians, and is a practical example of how valuable cooperation with other IB school librarians can be. Sharing good examples of previous years' essays is another example.

- Also investigate obtaining (from the IB publications center, via the IB website, or through your IBDP coordinator) a disc of 50 recommended examples of extended essays together with a new publication (due in fall 2010) that provides advice from examiners *IB Prepared: Approach Your Assessment the IB Way— Extended Essay*.

- Provide specific advice and guidance about citation and bibliography construction, as well as support in terms of the research process. Such advice may take the form of knowledge products, which may be web based, for instance, on a library web page or (depending on a school's ICT use policy) a Facebook or similar page. (Such library-generated products could also be useful for subject coursework requirements.) These could be comprehensive documents, or "short and sharp" in terms of just dealing with one point. Such short information sheets can be displayed around the library or put out handouts or leaflets that students can easily pick up and take away with them. Some examples of handouts are provided in Appendix 2.

- Help to ensure that students are aware of the dangers of plagiarism, and promote the concept of academic honesty (which is a focus of the following chapter). Make sure this advice is offered in a timely fashion. Some schools refer to academic honesty as honor codes, and students may be "required to turn a disk in or a receipt from Turnitin.com with the hard copy of the paper" (International Baccalaureate Mid-Atlantic Sub-Regional Coalition, 2006, MARC Best Practices section). It is equally important, as the IB itself says, that advice about plagiarism is not left until an extended or TOK essay is due to be handed in, but should be consistently reinforced (IBO, 2009).

- Make ongoing links with the local tertiary education library infrastructure, so that individual students can access resources in these facilities (and experience using such libraries). Think about involving a tutored visit to such facilities in company with the librarian or teachers; also facilitate reader tickets or similar privileges. This can be a positive factor for students, as it gives them experience of larger, complex libraries and helps alleviate possible "library anxiety" in university, where research indicated that students, once entering university, had "library anxiety" due to the size and complexity of libraries in tertiary education (Mellon, 1986).

- Be a supervisor for individual students. (As one example, the present writer was supervisor for a student who did an essay in ITGS, and who chose to evaluate a new management computer system for the school library.) It is best to check with your school's IBDP coordinator, but some schools require students to use teachers for the subjects that the school teaches, while other schools are more relaxed about this. A supervisor can be any member of the school staff, not just subject faculty.

- Offer short tutorial support (e.g., how to use databases) for individual students during any home room or tutorial time. Some U.S. librarians have offered classes or support during the summer holiday period between the first and second year of the IBDP, which is typically when students in the northern hemisphere are focusing on their essay.

- Make the essay the theme of a library open evening or "back to school" night, as some U.S. high schools have done.

- Ask IT students to make a video about how to use databases and any other aspect of the extended essay process that could involve the library. As we know, students tend to respect and value the views of their peers. Could such a project be deemed a CAS activity? It may be worth talking to the CAS coordinator about the possibility.

WORKING WITH THE IBDP COORDINATOR AND EXTENDED ESSAY SUPERVISORS

The activities outlined above are focused on interaction with students, either in a group or individually. It is crucial for the librarian to liaise with the IBDP coordinator, but it may also be useful to usefully liaise with individual extended essay supervisors. There may be occasions when the IBDP coordinator calls meetings or training sessions for supervisors, and the librarian could provide input (or simply attend). Input typically focuses on highlighting a supervisor's role in promoting good research habits and encouraging students to use a variety of resources to the best of their ability. As students remember what they use regularly and, as we have identified above, several requirements of the extended essay process will most likely be new to them, it will be helpful to students if the supervisor explicitly reminds and encourages students to use the library to help with their extended essay. During their regular meetings, a supervisor can ask the student the following questions:

- Have you checked whether the library has relevant information or resources to help focus the topic and the question?
- Have you used the catalog? What was the result? Could you find resources? Did you ask for help from the librarian to obtain specific items?
- Did you use online databases? Did you look at examples of previous extended essays in the library? Did you look at books about writing good essays? Did you try current periodicals, newspapers, DVDs (i.e., materials other than books)?
- Did you visit or use library webpages of relevant information and/or collect from the library help-sheets about the library role in the extended essay process?

It may be helpful to provide written information with the above information (or similar) so that a supervisor would have relevant information to hand to act as an *aide memoire* or rubric when meeting with a student. In other words, make it easy for supervisors to help students and the library.

THE LIBRARIAN IN THE EXTENDED ESSAY PROCESS

As a result of your interest in being involved in the extended essay process, you may be asked to become the extended essay coordinator for your school. Think carefully about this. It could be advantageous both to the library and students, but, equally there are a number of administrative aspects to such a role, and some clear deadlines that students need to comply with, and focusing on these could take away energies needed to develop library support to students. Also, if there is a financial aspect to taking on such a role, the "post" could have a political dimension in the organization, in which the library and librarian may become unwittingly involved, as it may be perceived as taking such a post away from a member of the regular teaching staff—sometimes these posts of extra responsibility are considered helpful to allow newer members of the profession to gain administrative experience. There are opportunities in the IBDP for the librarian to be seen in different ways by members of the school community (not least, of course, the students), nevertheless it is important that the librarian has a clear, core image.

PRACTICAL STRATEGIES FOR THE LIBRARIAN

- Liaise with the IBDP coordinator explicitly about supporting the extended essay *as a librarian*, and have clear ideas about what you can offer.

- Develop a library collection of previous years' examples of extended essays to help students see what is required, a typical format, and so forth.

- Make sure the latest IB guide for the extended essay is available in the library, and add various publications about essay writing.

- Produce knowledge products on essay writing/bibliography construction—in physical format and/or website based.

- Provide teaching support to students about researching, citation, and referencing, in some form. Ideally, this should begin in years prior to students becoming IBDP candidates.

- Discuss with the IBDP coordinator a possibility about holding specific seminars about library support for the essay process at an appropriate time for students.

- Facilitate access to local higher education institutions for students.

- Be involved in the process. Be a tutor for individual students (e.g., on developing good essay questions) or give resource advice to help guide students to suitable resources both in and out of the school.

- Investigate implications for provision and promote use of online databases, especially full-text databases.

- Prior to considering how the library could support the needs of students, check out unofficial, student-led websites about the extended essay (and "The IB-Extended Essay Procrastination" video on YouTube) to understand student views and concerns.

- In a school that offers pre-IB courses, program, or academy, recommend that the scope of the course includes coverage of inquiry and research skills, including citation and bibliography construction. This will be beneficial to students as there may be pressure of time for these aspects once they have started the IBDP, and these skills will be valuable not only for the extended essay but also for other aspects of the diploma.

- Liaise and provide support and information for extended essay supervisors.

- Consider offering an online help/support service for students, especially if they are developing an extended essay during a long (typically, summer) vacation from school.

5

THE IB LEARNER PROFILE
AND ACADEMIC HONESTY

This chapter concentrates on two important IB documents that relate to all the IB programs but none more so than the IBDP. For librarians, information literacy is relevant to both the learner profile and academic honesty.

THE LEARNER PROFILE

The importance of the learner profile in IB thinking cannot be underestimated. This document identifies learning qualities and attributes in a holistic manner. The profile is an outline of a student learner continuum throughout the three programs of the IB, and beyond. In terms of the IBDP, it may be helpful for librarians especially to think of it in relation to critical, digital, and information literacies, as well as teaching and learning styles.

The IB learner profile document was developed in 2006. Its importance is reflected in the fact that it is reproduced at the beginning of each official IB curriculum document. There are 10 elements, which are that IB students should be:

- Inquirers
- Knowledgeable
- Thinkers
- Communicators
- Principled
- Open-minded
- Caring
- Risk-takers
- Balanced
- Reflective

The generic descriptors or explanation about each aspect or quality listed above are available in the learner profile document, together with suggestions for implementing and monitoring the use of the learner profile in individual schools. Librarians should familiarize themselves with this document, which is available on the OCC.

It would be helpful for librarians to reflect on how to use the learner profile in the library. A first step may be writing descriptors for each quality in the library, for example-

> Thinker—*What do you think of information you have just read, whether on line or in print? Is it reliable? Can you trust it?*
>
> Risk-taker—*Why not try that book you just glanced at!*
>
> Reflective—*What skills have you learned over time about using information and resources in the library? By reflecting, you may find that you know more than you think about finding out information!*
>
> Inquirer—*What do you want to find out more about that item on the news broadcast? You're in the right place for inquiry...*
>
> Caring—*Are there any people around you in the library? How can you care for their environment and personal space?*
>
> Principled—*Have you acknowledged every source of information you've used in your own work?*
>
> Open-minded—*Are you open to new ideas and ways and habits of learning?*
>
> Balanced—*Have you given equal weight and looked at both sides of an issue in your work?*
>
> Communicators—*Is a shrug effective communication?*
>
> Knowledgeable—*Did you know that using a research process can help you to be knowledgeable?*

Librarians have produced their own learner profile descriptors, and a check on the Internet on Glogster or a school's own website should produce examples. Some people have taken a questioning approach, whilst others have provided more detailed comments or statements about what they think the learner profile elements mean in a school library context. At any rate, taking on board the learner profile elements and localizing their relevance means that the learner profile becomes more real, and not just a paper statement. If a library spin or take on the learner profile elements is used in a visual form in the library, it may be worth having more than one comment for each element, so that they can be refreshed regularly. Another possibility is using learner profile statements on a carousel of slides that could be displayed on a wall-mounted visual display unit.

It is helpful to reflect on the skills that students need in order to successfully navigate the IBDP. Generally in IBDP, there is a focus on research about skills that students need, and IB secondary literature promotes an inquiry and research way of working for students. However, there is a singular lack of reference in these studies and commentaries to libraries and librarians, suggesting that library models in this curriculum do not correspond to that recommended in LIS *professional* literature.

Tension may exist between an understanding of the IBDP as a process vehicle, and as a traditional, content-rich curriculum. This latter view may conflict with promotion of a model of school libraries, whose utility is based on an acceptance of constructivism, though this has not always been acknowledged in the past. In developing information literacy, it is important that librarians understand pedagogy (Hepworth & Walton, 2009). In such a demanding curriculum as IBDP (Vanderbrook, 2006; Yip, 2000), with time and workload pressures (Taylor, Pogrebin, & Dodge, 2002), students may not have time to use a library. Some researchers indicate they may not need to do so. Earning good grades through content-rich lecture style teaching (Kyburg, Hertberg-Davis, & Callahan, 2007) and using the IBDP to enter better universities, with significant scaffolding provided by teachers (Burris, Welner, Wiley, & Murphy, 2007) may negate any perceived use of a school library (i.e., such structured support may not allow for or require independent study through a library). Why this should be may be explained by the following factors:

- Libraries and librarians do not significantly feature in IBO documentation, not least—*crucially*—in IBDP subject documentation.
- Libraries do not feature in writings of IB commentators or practitioners.
- Lack of teacher education in library use as an aspect of pedagogy, or experience of good practice.
- Reliance on textbooks for IBDP subjects (of which there are an increasing number) and/or the Internet.

These factors are challenges for the IBDP school librarian to overcome. However, skills have been identified in IBDP subject and core documentation, and skills (even if sometimes only in general terms) have been mentioned in the writings of various commentators (Andain, Rutherford, & Allen, 2006; Anderson, 1994; Coffey, 2006; Croft & Cross, 2003; Drake, 2004; Fox, 1998; Hill, 2003; Mathews & Hill, 2005; Spahn, 2001). Indeed, research undertaken by the present writer in 2005 found that the following skills and qualities were identified in extant IBDP documents.

- Critical thinking/reading/analysis
- Personal communication skills
- Learning skills/inquiry skills
- Higher-order thinking
- Reasoning skills
- Personal reflection
- Independent working
- Working cooperatively/team work
- Decision-making
- Confidence, independence, maturity, tolerance, open-mindedness
- Personal knowledge
- Asking and answering own questions
- Responsibility
- Creative thinking
- Study skills/information literacy/study habits/academic rigor

- Synthesize information/note-taking
- Self-discipline
- Planning skills
- Time management
- Writing skills
- Research skills
- Understanding and applying logic
- Discrimination (between truth and opinion)
- Emotional intelligence

The school librarian must work diligently to link both library and librarian to these skills and their perception by students. For the future of students in universities, these skills should not be overlooked because of time limitations associated with teaching considerable content. Information literacy skills must be pointed out as relevant in a content transference model of learning. Even if some areas of the IBDP are more inquiry based, there is concern that skills are only implicit and limited to TOK and the extended essay (Stobie, 2005, 2007). If a number of students only take the certificate version, teachers and students may not perceive of any need, requirement, or experience with information literacy skills. There is, though, an exception in terms of time management and prioritization skills. Nevertheless, Kyburg et al. (2007) indicated that students need good levels of a broad range of skills and aptitudes, including motivation, *before* commencing the diploma program.

Librarians have promoted research skills (Lear, 2002) though noting from their perspective, there is a lack of identification of information literacy in IBDP documentation (Brown & Laverty, 2001); and Clark (1995) alluded to library anxiety that students may encounter when entering tertiary education. Students thought IBDP could be or was stressful (Burke, 2005; Paris, 2003; Yip, 2000), and pressures encountered required support (Burris et al., 2007). Such stress and pressures could result in plagiarism (Taylor et al., 2002). In order to succeed in the IBDP, students needed to develop various skills to cope and manage (Kyburg et al., 2007; Snapper, 2006), not least time management skills (Taylor & Porath, 2006; Tekle, 2005; Vanderbrook, 2006). A more recent study of underrepresented groups in magnet IBDPs found that it was helpful to prepare students for the IBDP with appropriate content and skills either through following the MYP or pre-IB courses (Bland & Woodworth, 2009).

Research looked at various broad areas or domains that were focused on skills or learning styles/qualities. This study, by the IB Global Policy and Research Team, in collaboration with the Center for Evaluation and Education Policy at Indiana University, found by looking at IB and non-IB students from eight high schools, that IB students rated their levels of attainment as higher in several domain areas: cognitive, intellectual, and academic engagement; social, behavioral, and participatory engagement, and emotional engagement. In relation to the present discussion, the cognitive/academic domain included specific items such as asking students how many hours they spent per week on reading and studying for classes, the extent that they were engaged in class discussions, how often they undertook research beyond set or assigned texts, and how often students made connections between classes or subject areas (IBO, 2010b).

RESULTS OF THE IBDP LIBRARY STUDY IN RELATION TO INFORMATION LITERACY

There is a considerable literature concerning information literacy and school libraries. Did the writer's study specifically about the IBDP reflect published research? Perhaps overall general findings in the published research could readily transfer to an IBDP context. However, the study found that there were exceptions and distinctions to be made in relation to the IBDP.

The study certainly found that bibliography and citation skills were required and valued by students, most obviously for the extended essay, but also for coursework in nearly all IBDP subject requirements; however, in practice, this varied according to the subjects chosen by students. Teachers and administrators in the study thought the skills applied to all major areas of the IBDP.

With regard to plagiarism, teachers' views, awareness, and concern varied depending on subject specialism. For instance, group 2 (languages) and group 4 (sciences) said that because of group and class work, plagiarism was not likely to occur, and if it did, identifying it was straightforward. For other groups, it was a major concern. Strategies used by some teachers included requiring students to provide bibliographies and accurate in-text citation of sources. Teachers, however, did not identify a specific role for the librarian with regard to plagiarism, which is at variance with the trend in LIS literature, though not from non-LIS literature on plagiarism. However, as there was little, if any time for students in an IBDP to substantially develop skills, teachers thought that students needed to obtain the skills prior to commencing IBDP, specifically in middle or junior high school.

There was also a common assumption among teachers that students could sift, evaluate, and choose relevant information from a variety of sources; however, on reflection, they found that this could be an erroneous assumption. This also applied when students thought that teachers assumed that they (students) could and would use the library for assignments, whereas this may not have been the case. Here, it was important for teachers to articulate their expectations, and not assume that students would use the library without specific encouragement.

What did the study find were the most important skills for IBDP? Teachers thought these were time management, research skills, and critical thinking. Teachers discussed the broad findings about skills from research with former IBDP students by Hayden, Rancic, and Thompson (2000). Whereas Hayden and colleagues identified a broader range of intangible and tangible factors, the present study found more focused attention to students' abilities to successfully pursue and manage an academic program. These more specific attributes also reflected findings of studies related to the IBDP, (e.g., Qualifications & Curriculum Authority, 2003) and especially some North American studies (Burris et al., 2007; Kyburg et al., 2007; Taylor et al., 2002).

In information literacy literature, there is more emphasis on intellectual-higher-order thinking skills than on time management, whereas literature specifically related to plagiarism suggests that poor time management is a relevant factor, together with pressure of workload. Grade 12 students and teachers both highlighted time management as possibly *the* most important skill, reflecting findings of Latrobe and Havenar (1997) and a IBDP study (Taylor & Porath, 2006). Closely allied were prioritizing work and the need to memorize considerable content. Students therefore developed note-taking skills. They also developed research skills, mainly through the experience of the extended essay requirement.

Were bibliography and citation skills important in practice? Students had various experiences concerning applying bibliography and citation skills. Most students and teachers thought they needed them as coursework applied to all IBDP subject areas as well as core elements. A few students only used them for extended and possibly TOK essays, reflecting work by Stobie, who concluded that skills were only implicit in the IBDP (2005) and that research skills were required only for extended essay purposes (2007).

Who taught students these skills? Students, teachers, and administrators in the study all referred to the librarian teaching, modeling, and advising about these skills. The librarian's role in this case could be regarded as a leadership role. This reflects LIS literature (e.g., Farmer, 2005; McGregor & Streitenburger, 1998) because members of the IBDP school community saw the librarian as having strong expertise in referencing. This is possibly not least because it could be regarded as tangible, concrete, and discrete, thereby more easily comprehended, and was related to a product, the essay, or coursework.

When should students be taught these skills? In the present study, teachers and students considered that students needed a history of skill development and practice in using those skills and in library use before beginning IBDP because of the time pressures in the program. This was especially true of bibliography and in-text citation skills, and some teachers recommended a standardized style as being helpful for mixed-ability groups. While not identifying citation skills, Kyburg et al. (2007), in an IBDP study, similarly found that students needed a heritage of study and information-handling and research skills in order to meet the demands of the IBDP.

What does IBDP subject documentation say about the role of the library? Several teachers noted the lack of an explicit statement of a role for the library in IB subject documentation. If explicit directions were included in the documentation, teachers might be more likely to consider and possibly include library use and the skills that students need to effectively use the library as part of their teaching strategies. One teacher was very specific about subject documentation, as this was where he would and did look. This mirrors conclusions of Pratt (1994) that there was a dichotomy between expectations of school libraries as expressed in LIS role statements and the lack of meaningful reference in curricular documentation and a lack of synergy between the literatures of education and school librarianship (Montiel-Overall, 2005).

How can the library be involved in the motivation of students? Administrators especially promoted the view of self-motivation of students. One teacher specifically referred to the learner profile when commenting on students grasping the initiative and reading around the subject on their own initiative without needing to be given it as an assignment. Some students noted that they used the library on their own initiative, and this was an example of motivation. Kyburg et al. (2007) found that IBDP students were organized, with good levels of skills (which they needed to develop before starting IBDP), and motivated. LIS studies (Latrobe & Havenar, 1997; Scott & Owings, 2005) indicated that motivated students could successfully access an information-rich environment, but teachers noted that less able (less motivated) students did not use such a range of resources. It may be therefore that the library in the study, as an independent learning environment, attracted, related to, and supported more able and motivated students who could use it more effectively. These more able and motivated students, who could use libraries independently, fitted a more traditional profile of IBDP candidates. The challenge arises with students who do not fit the traditional profile but still undertake the IBDP. That such students need support was borne out by Burris et al. (2007), and Todd (2003) and others note a librarian's role in providing scaffolding and support for some students. This may indicate a different role for the librarian in relation to less able students.

What skills do students need in using a library? Students may more readily use a library if they are more comfortable and secure in using skills to do so. Students, when asked, considered they could do so (Streatfield & Markless, 1994; and, remembering that this is a study of IBDP students in an international school, Latuputty, 2005). However, from an adult perspective, students had limited awareness and skills in how libraries and databases worked (Limberg & Alexandersson, 2003). In the present study though, overall students showed a realistic appraisal of their skills in using the library, which varied among students, but may have something to do with the fact that it was their librarian who asked them this question.

Generally speaking, students may not be able to carry out basic university research (Daniel, 1997; Ellis & Salisbury, 2004) but, once they have arrived in tertiary education, they somehow manage to find strategies to bridge the gap themselves (Fitzgerald & Galloway, 2003). At school, students would only develop skills if they were set or encouraged to undertake challenging research tasks (Langford, 1998). In theory, the extended essay could provide that experience. A premise that analysis, formal essay presentation, evaluation, and critical thinking were all skills that should be developed by senior students (Goodin, 1991; Riedling, 2004) suggests that these skills could be catered for by a student's experience of extended and TOK essays. In the IBDP, good levels of confidence of individual students who could readily transfer skills was also important (Hayden & Wong, 1997; Munro, 2003; Stobie, 2005, 2007).

For research skills in particular, some evidence suggests that research skills are most relevant to the extended essay (Qualifications & Curriculum Authority, 2003; Stobie, 2007). However, the only studies to link any library involvement and contributions to the process are practitioner librarian studies (Latuputty, 2005; Tilke, 2009). Therefore, the main skills needed by students were time management, prioritization, developing strategies to cope with significant amounts of content, research skills, and citation/bibliography skills.

What about their Internet-searching skills? Because students use the Internet every day, it might be assumed that students are sophisticated users of electronic information. However, in this study, several students reflected that their skills improved in a trial-and-error way, such as the limited search terms they initially used (which indicated little use of critical thinking). Teachers too noted students' limited skills and strategies in using the Internet, which reflects Combes and Sekulla (2002) and Scott and Owings (2005) and several later studies, including Rowlands and Nicholas (2008).

In conclusion, it may be considered that the present study (and indeed other non-LIS IBDP studies) suggest that students fall short of the learner profile aims. That would be too sweeping a statement, not the least in the absence of research about students and their full learner profile attainments in the IBDP. What these studies do show is that some aspects have developed and that others need to be worked on. The learner profile is a major IB statement about learning processes and outcomes, qualities, and attributes that students should have in and through adult life, and it is that continuum that is important. It is unrealistic to think or expect that students will have good levels of skills and attainment in all aspects of the learner profile by 18 years of age. Indeed, the IB considers that this is a set of principles, skills, and attitudes *for life*, and IBDP students are only beginning their adult life. It is therefore relevant to think of the learner profile as not so much an information literacy pillar of the program, but as a stage along a person's journey in life, and one in which the school library may make a discrete impact or contribution, together with other aspects of school life.

ACADEMIC HONESTY

It is fitting that this follows a discussion of the IB learner profile, as the profile is a positive statement of what a learner looks like. The term, "academic honesty" is itself relevant and important as it stresses the positive, rather than simply focusing on a negative aspect: plagiarism, important though that is. The IB has developed an important document specifically for the IBDP that outlines recommended practice related to this concept. For librarians, the document contains information and identifies strategies and relationships to promote the importance of ethical research, citation, and student understanding of plagiarism. Teaching the importance of academic honesty can positively feed into some of the more general aspects of the learner profile identified above (e.g.. thinker, balanced, carer, reflective, principled).

THE IB ACADEMIC HONESTY DOCUMENT

For the IB, academic honesty is a formal aspect of the IBDP and is governed by a document, which is regularly updated. This section of the book comments on a document that was issued in July 2009. The current document is always available at the academic honesty section of the OCC. Librarians in IBDP schools should be familiar with the latest version of the document, so always check the version on the OCC. To support the work of the IB in this important area, the IB created a new post in 2010, that of academic honesty manager, who is based at the IB Curriculum and Assessment Center.

The document defines "academic honesty," establishes roles and responsibilities of those involved and offers advice to a school on preventing and detecting "malpractice." The document promotes values and skills that "promote integrity and good practice in teaching, learning and assessment" (p. 2).

Students should understand various terms and concepts, such as the difference between collaboration, cooperation, and collusion. In terms of authentic work, the document acknowledges the creative cycle, so that new ideas and work derives from earlier work, but the acknowledgement must be made clear. Students must understand that the same conventions apply for information that is considered to be in the public domain. It discusses paraphrasing, and the need for both in-text citation and bibliography entry.

The IB document should not be used instead of a school's own policy as "every IB world school . . . [should have] a policy to promote academic honesty" (section 4.2., p. 8). A school's own policy should refer to the IB learner profile and IB definitions of plagiarism, collusion and duplication of work. Because a policy should be a practical document, it should also include advice and examples of what constitutes academic *dis*honesty, and "examples of conventions for citing and acknowledging original authorship" (s. 4.6, p. 9), and by so doing promotes good practice.

The academic honesty document acknowledges that sometimes students have an inability to source material they have used, indeed "many candidates are not aware of when or how to acknowledge sources. It is essential that candidates are taught this important academic skill" (s. 2.4, p. 4).

Probably out of all the IBDP documentation, a librarian's role is most clearly outlined in this document, which states that "the role and expertise of the school librarian must not be neglected." The document recognizes that the training of librarians means that they are familiar with issues to do with copyright and the dangers of plagiarism, and have rigorous high standards of research themselves. The document recommends that the librarian should "provide research guidelines," so that students may have sufficient information to enable them to practice established academic procedures. Thereby, students could produce "well-written work that does not rely heavily on material downloaded from the Internet." According to this document, "locating, evaluating and using information are skills characteristic of a librarian's profession in addition to those offered by teachers" (section 4.9).

Apart from the librarian, other adults in the school have a role to play too, including parents and guardians, who can promote good standards and practice. The role of teachers in making students aware of appropriate conventions is identified, and this particularly applies to extended essay supervisors. In practice, there may be a range of adults that the school librarian needs to liaise with and perhaps educate in specific skills.

In essence, the question of which convention or system for citation that the IB recommends is dealt with by section 4.11, which acknowledges that a convention for citation must be used, however a particular method is not specified. A school, a teacher, or a student can choose one, but that system must be applied consistently. It is a recommendation that students should use 'thoroughly resourced online libraries of books and journals [i.e. subscription databases, which] enables candidates (and teachers) to keep notes that are properly referenced' (s. 4.15, p. 10), which may refer to the fact that full bibliographic details are provided with each source and perhaps to features on some databases that enable individual students to create a bibliography. The IB also recommends use of web-based detection services, such as www.Turnitin.com, to help students and teachers with ensuring high standards of academic honesty are maintained.

PRACTICAL STRATEGIES FOR THE LIBRARIAN

- Work with the IBDP coordinator, who should be aware of specific rules and procedures to be employed in relation to issues of academic honesty.
- Develop knowledge products about citation methods.
- Lead a course or team teach bibliography and citation in an overt and timely manner to students.
- Be involved in developing and promoting a school academic honesty policy.

- Promote the idea of a continuum of skills development, so that students are introduced to the skills of bibliography-construction and in-text citation in middle school years.

- Work with teachers and curriculum leaders so that these skills are valued and assessed.

- Provide courses or information for IBDP teachers, especially extended essay supervisors, about bibliography/citation skills.

- Liaise with the IBDP coordinator and others to discuss whether it would be better for a particular school to adopt a particular referencing style or method, or acknowledge that different methods are more suitable for different subject areas. Once this decision has been made, it should be communicated to the faculty, and included in basic information that is passed on to new members of faculty.

- Maintain a section in the school library of relevant materials about ethical research (both in general collections in the library as well as any collection maintained specifically for teachers).

- Develop content on a library webpage or school intranet about research skills, and have it linked to other school pages.

- Provide group or individual tutorial support to students in the researching phase and writing phase of their concluding project and other coursework.

- Check the OCC for the latest version of the learner profile document, and be familiar with this document; also check the academic honesty page of the OCC.

- Make up your own library descriptors for learner profile elements; perhaps use Glogster or a similar product to make your own posters featuring the learner profile.

- Make explicit reference to the learner profile in your school library documents, including a collection development policy that has been validated at school board level. This document may also feed into a statement about freedom of information.

- Compile a display or promotion around banned books in order to generate an awareness and/or discussion about freedom of information and ideas.

- Check out Noodletools.com's "Template for a Plagiarism Policy: Goals of an Ethics Policy" (see http://www.noodletools.com/debbie/ethical/policytemplate.html) for a good policy template.

6

---·◆·---

HOW DO IBDP STUDENTS
USE THE SCHOOL LIBRARY?

This chapter looks at needs, practices, and habits of grade (G) 11 and 12 students, that is, students identified in the general research literature and from the present IBDP research study. Typically these students are 16–18 years of age. The chapter identifies (a) what, if anything, these students want from school libraries; (b) how these students want and get their information; and (c) strategies the librarian can use to support the information needs of IBDP candidates.

OLDER STUDENT NEEDS AND USE OF LIBRARIES

Studies that observed student behavior, interviewed students and others, were mostly small scale and based on real on-going situations (rather than planned, formal research projects). These studies showed there was a clear indication that the library was regarded as a place for study (e.g., Spreadbury & Spiller, 1999; Streatfield & Markless, 1994). A quiet environment may be valued as a place of study, but a library can also be territorial and social in function (Shilling & Cousins, 1990). Whether this was because of facilities being limited elsewhere in school may not always be clear, and in some studies, there was no indication that schools did not regard their library as simply somewhere the students had to be when not being taught (Rafste, 2003, 2005; Shoham & Shemer-Shalman, 2003). In such situations, the role of librarians changed from resource provider and facilitator to that of disciplinarian and rule-enforcer (Frew, 2006; KRC Research, 2003; Limberg & Alexandersson, 2003). Sometimes, the school library was regarded as a pleasant place to be, and because students felt is was a pleasant place to be, the library was felt to be separate from the school itself (KRC Research, 2003).

Provision of space as a main library use has been routinely identified in role statements, such as guidelines and other documents from the LIS sector, though there may have been an assumption that the library was that space where library resources would be used by students. However, studies showed that use of (traditional) resources was a secondary use, though that place, because of availability of and access to technology outside the library (e.g., in a wireless environment), was relative.

It is presently being suggested that technology *can* make both library and librarian role invisible or redundant (Limberg & Alexandersson, 2003). Internet use in particular is a natural part of young people's lives, so a library can seem anachronistic and irrelevant (Levin & Arafeh, 2002). A disparity may exist between student views of their own skills base and views of librarians and others (Combes & Sekulla, 2002; Scott & Owings, 2005; Streatfield & Markless, 1994; Williamson, McGregor, Archibald, & Sullivan, 2007). Rowlands and Nicholas (2008) identified a role for adults in helping students, whereas students themselves may not see the need for such assistance, but their study about the information behavior of the researcher of the future found that young people were not necessarily web literate. They relied too heavily on search engines, viewed rather than read webpages, and had not developed critical skills to assess information they found on websites. For slightly older (college) students, as part of Project Information Literacy, Head and Eisenberg (2009) found that digital research was more challenging and difficult and highlighted students lack of relevant skills. Although this led to frustration, "students valued libraries, and librarians, especially in assisting them with their strategies for retrieving 'citable stuff' and helping them navigate complex information spaces" (p. 10).

Students do study and they need to study, but research reports suggested that the focus of their study needs to be examined. The question remains: what did they study, and what did they use to help them study? After all, content from taught classes, supplemented by textbooks, may have been sufficient to earn them good marks (as Rafste [2003] found in Norway). Textbooks may have assumed a greater importance, possibly obviating any need for independent research (Madden, Ford, & Miller, 2007), and, as one study found, textbooks specifically limited library use (Spreadbury & Spiller, 1999). While a later study (Williamson et al., 2007) noted the prevalence of the Internet as a convenient source of information, students still highly valued subject textbooks. This implied students using the library as a place of study, but bringing their own resources (often only textbooks) with them.

When this is the situation, information literacy, highly recommended by the LIS sector, may not seem or be relevant. Indeed, there is little research evidence to link a school librarian with student acquisition of information literacy skills (as Lonsdale's [2003] meta-analysis for the Australian School Library Association found). Although LIS secondary or professional literature urges such a role, Moore (2005) points out that, historically, such input has been ineffective. This situation can only be overcome when librarians show teachers and students the value of using libraries to find accurate and relevant information. It is important to show how librarians can have cutting-edge knowledge of new databases and other information.

Unsurprisingly, teachers have been identified as the most important source of information for students (Irving, 2006; Latrobe & Havener, 1997). It is no surprise to note that research suggests how teachers teach could be considered a limiting factor on use of libraries. Didactic teaching practices have been identified (Spreadbury & Spiller, 1999; Streatfield & Markless, 1994), and associated with the need to teach significant amounts of subject content to comply with the needs of external examinations. Teachers feel time pressures in transmitting significant amounts of content to students (Williams & Wavell, 2006). Although exact practices vary between teachers and the subjects they teach, students are often directly provided with information they need (Merchant & Hepworth, 2002), thereby limiting library use.

When students need information, they rely on the Internet (McLelland & Crawford, 2004; Williamson et al., 2007) not only for academic information but also socially (Levin & Arafeh, 2002; Rafste, 2005). Internet use is a natural part of their lives, and as digital natives, students feel they are adept at finding and using information found on the Internet. This is a view not necessarily shared by teachers or librarians who understand that much of the information retrieved is neither accurate nor relevant. Student use does not generally extend to database use (Barranoik, 2001; Limberg & Alexandersson, 2003). Although database use continues to be promoted by librarians (Wright & Christine, 2006), the use of databases must begin with teaching teachers about databases and having them make assignments that will get the students to use databases. The school library online catalog is also rarely used (Frew, 2006; Spreadbury & Spiller, 1999). When students do use libraries, they generally need to ask a librarian to find information/resources.

Expectations are that students will require sophisticated levels of information literacy to succeed or even survive in higher education, and, not least in the professional literature, this is based on a belief that learning is constructivist, in which the research process is important (Branch & Oberg, 2001). Therefore a possible contradiction between a constructivist pedagogy advocated by librarians and use of other pedagogy by teachers may result (Williams & Wavell, 2006). A question arises as to whether skills developed in secondary education are useful in tertiary education (Ellis & Salisbury, 2004).

In an early LIS grounded theory study, Mellon (1986) developed a concept of library anxiety, where students were doubtful of their own abilities and over-awed by the complex size of university libraries. Students needed confidence to overcome such obstacles (Goodin, 1991), but Daniel (1997) observed limited abilities to do more than basic research, and students in school used resources as directed by teachers (Langford, 1998), which suggests that students had limited research experience prior to university. One consequence of limited skills may be a tendency to plagiarize (Williamson et al., 2007). The temptation to plagiarize may be due to considerable workload (Millard, 2005); and external examination syllabus requirements and pressures (Boden & Carroll, 2006). However, the pressure could be limited by scaffolding provided by teachers and librarians; at any rate, students developed skills over time at university, valuing them more, and gaining confidence (Kuhlthau, 2004). It is important to note that some positive links have been found between school and tertiary education (e.g., Smalley, 2004).

WHAT THIS STUDY OF THE LIBRARY IN THE IBDP FOUND

Because the few studies of IBDP and the school library focused on specific aspects (Latuputty's case study in 2005 concentrated on the post–extended essay period, and Rafste [2003] included one library where the IBDP was offered, though the focus of the research was on the socialization aspect of the library rather than as a support for a particular curriculum), the study of the present writer is one that focuses on use of the library as a support to the IBDP overall. This research involved considerable formal observation of students in the library and interviewed students' one year into the program, as well as following up with the same students after they had finished IBDP.

An interesting distinction is that this study was in a school where *all* the G11 and G12 students undertook the program. It was not an option for a select group, such as gifted students, as may occur in a number of schools. At the school in the study, the IBDP was the curriculum for all students aged 16–18 years, and it was very rare that a student undertook only the certificate option; virtually all completed the whole diploma requirements. This is not apparently an unusual occurrence for IBDP provision throughout the world.

It is important to stress that the present IBDP study, though one of impact, is not a study that can necessarily be used in the way that impact studies have been used (i.e., as an advocacy tool). Here, the impact is seen in a real situation, by real students and teachers. When undertaking such naturalistic, qualitative research, librarians need to accept that findings are not always as one would wish. (Indeed, it would have been possible to set up a particular project, say of IBDP subject/ library involvement, library support for the extended essay, or use of the library by TOK students in the library, that could have produced very different results.) The results that librarians get from research can tell librarians about what their faculty and students think about library support and can provide evidence upon which to make changes. Additionally, given that there is at present a very small research base of library practice and impact on the IBDP, there are opportunities for librarians to contribute reports about small IBDP/library–related research, so that there will be a greater body of relevant literature to help IBDP librarians in the future. So, even if some of the findings presented below seem negative, they can be used as factors on which to reflect and evaluate the library of the reader's own institution, and as stepping-stones for future research into the school library and the IBDP.

What Did IBDP Students Do in the School Library?

From observation, most students' used the library as a space to sit and study; they came largely to complete assignments, read, and write. For the most part, they used textbooks, materials, and equipment that were provided by students themselves and/or their teachers. The most-used library "resource" was a laptop computer (Mac iBook) that individual students could borrow from the library, for use in the library and elsewhere. The library held a number of these computers, which students could borrow for individual periods. In the library, students used iBooks to access the Internet, to word process, to listen to music (as an aid to study), and for e-mailing. Use of all other library resources was the third most–observed use, overall. This included students browsing the shelves; reading books, magazines, and newspapers; and viewing library-stocked DVDs in a library classroom. Nevertheless, use of library resources did not normally extend to borrowing (except for iBooks).

Disrupting talk and use of the library as primarily a social area was not identified as a significant observed activity, though low-level chat was observed. Students tended to use what seating they wanted, whether easy chairs or study carrels, and the type of seating did not dictate or encourage the type of activity they engaged in. If they wanted to chat or talk while in a group situation, they did so in easy chairs or from carrels. If they wanted to work individually, again they did so, irrespective of the type or sort of seating chosen. However, informal group use was another regular activity of students in the library. This was either ad hoc by students themselves, in small groups for classes with a teacher, and for CAS activities and meetings with supervisors.

Students infrequently asked the library staff for help. (It should be noted that, during the observed period, the librarian ran a series of seminars about research and citation in the extended essay, which may have made potential questions unnecessary.) The library catalog was rarely consulted by students. Students who used the library voluntarily appeared methodical and managed their time well, though a minority could not settle (evidenced by short attention spans) alternating with chatting and moving around the library, and visiting the library ICT area.

Observation, therefore, suggested that library use related to use of library space, followed by ICT and library resources. These observations formed themes for semistructured questions in interviews with students. Several G11 students (i.e., those in the first year of their IBDP candidature) were interviewed at the end of their G11 year and again at the end of the G12 year, at the end of their two-year IBDP course. Several G12 students were also interviewed in the first year of the research, in order to provide a comparison.

What Did G11 Students Think of the Library?

The students overall thought that the school library could offer a quiet environment that may be helpful to aid their study. One student used the library as a matter of course or habit, whereas another preferred the quietest area of the library for "serious study . . . where I can really concentrate." The study included students who did not use the library, and some preferred a more social atmosphere that was available to them when they were not being taught in other parts of the school. They also preferred to study later in the day, at home, sometimes socially, with friends. All students therefore made choices about where to study and what constituted study. Students also had a need for socializing, perhaps to ease pressure or seek group support for their overall workload or particular assignments.

Library use as part of required assignments was limited and teacher encouragement varied, according to students. Students all had different experiences. One thought that most teachers "encourage us to use the library," whereas, at the other extreme, another considered that "they don't bother" because the Internet was used all the time. Yet another student felt that any teacher encouragement of the library "was more for specific assignments." When asked, students who had used the library for assignments were unable to suggest any required assessment of use of library resources.

All students could recall using physical library resources during the first year of their IBDP candidature, though the variety and extent varied: general interest books; reference and nonfiction materials; encyclopedias; periodicals; DVDs; and fiction books were all mentioned. Most students had used the library catalog and sometimes asked librarians for help to locate items, though again this varied. One student actually preferred to "walk around and look at the sections," and thus developed a self-help, independent approach. However, those students who used the catalog needed time to think about the question, and only one student used the catalog regularly. All students had used ICT resources and facilities, and this was especially true of laptop computers. Fewer students had used subscription databases, and only one used the library webpage and valued the information about citation and referencing that he found there. Internet use was, however, universal and regular.

Students were asked to reflect on various qualities associated with the IBDP, and more students considered that time management skills were the most important as "there is a lot of work; for me being able to plan my time and work individually has been very important for getting things done on time" said one student. Other aspects students thought important were independent study skills and critical thinking. At this stage of IBDP, students had finished their first year and were just starting on the extended essay process, several students thought the library could support subject studies, as well as core areas. However, a couple of students thought that the library was more of a help for the core, and the extended essay at that. Some students noted that they felt that provision of previous years' extended essays as examples in the library was the library's main contribution. All students regarded teachers and textbooks as most important information sources for their IBDP needs. Other sources, such as library, home, and Internet, followed, but precise order varied. This then was the situation for students half way through their IBDP candidature.

What Did Students Who Had Finished the Program Think of the Library?

At the same time as interviewing G11 students, the librarian as researcher also asked students at the end of G12 for their impressions of the library in terms of their IBDP experiences. In terms of a study environment, several G12 students used the library and appreciated the quiet; but this depended on the personality of the student. Others needed collegiality, socialization, and peer support. A difference was the use of the library to help alleviate stress; according to one student, "if I was stressed out, I'd relax for a few minutes before the next lesson." This was partly due to an enjoyment of physical personal space, less distraction, and the chance to focus. All the students interviewed were aware of the perceived environment of the library, and used it according to need and inclination. Students needed breaks from study and tended not to study during lunch break, recess, or after school, partly because students needed to fit in activities, CAS, and sports commitments.

Some G12 students had used the library as part of subject-based assignments. Some remembered a need to produce bibliographies as a result of researching in the library. Other students had not used or been required to use the library during their G12 year. Subject use varied, but examples among social sciences, arts, and English (IBDP groups 1, 3, and 6) were mentioned and especially coursework (internal assessment) for history.

Time management was again considered the most important aspect of the IBDP by virtually all G12 students interviewed, and became more important as the G12 year progressed. They felt that research skills were important, as all coursework required research.

Students who used the library as a place to study also used library resources both for academic and recreational use. Of IBDP use, library use for extended essay needs was common, though one increased his use of resources in G12 as "all coursework requires research" and another used "kids books on history" to help review for final examinations. ICT/Internet use was common, and more students used subscription databases and consulted library information about citation and bibliography construction, which was available on the library webpage. More used the catalog during the year, though the extent varied as did students' ability to locate resources on library shelves, and students all asked staff for help in finding resources, including one student (who said he knew where to look, as he had been a CAS helper in the library) who asked for help "sometimes now in lazy moments." More students in G12 asked the librarian for advice and help relating to general questions about creating bibliographies for extended and TOK essays, but some asked for help concerning identifying and obtaining resources for individual extended essays.

Students had varied perceptions concerning encouragement from teachers to use the library during their G12 year. Several students suggested that teachers of English, history, and TOK, which one student referred to as book-related subjects, encouraged students to use the library. One student mentioned an English teacher who required students to visit the library and "find ten books and do a bibliography of them." The student found that this was a useful exercise, not only for the class, but "was important especially for the extended essay and college" application essays. The remaining students thought of encouragement in terms of general exhortation. One student had a theory that teachers believed students made extensive use of the Internet, therefore teachers recommending use of the library was a corrective measure.

Student perception of the library's potential to help with various aspects of the IBDP varied, though all mentioned extended essays and TOK essays. For subject use, students were divided. Half of them thought that the Internet was sufficient or that the library was not relevant, not least because information was provided directly by teachers and through textbooks; some students disagreed with this. Students did not identify many subjects where this was the case, but all noted that for science and mathematics courses, all their information came through teachers and textbooks. However, history was commonly cited as a subject where library use was helpful.

Some students associated the image of the library with books and preferred this because it reflected their personality style and a belief that book-based information was more authoritative. However, when asked to rank sources of information in terms of importance to them, teachers and textbooks were regarded as most important by all G12 students interviewed. The term *textbooks* has been known to be used imprecisely, so it is important to say that students understood the term textbook to be those books given to them by teachers for various IBDP subject areas. Some of textbooks used were written and published expressly for the IBDP. One student voiced a common belief that textbooks were most of value "because they are specifically for the IB, they are written by IB examiners, so are helpful."

How Did the Two Groups of Students Compare and Differ?

Use of the school library for study varied among G11 and G12 students. Both groups made choices about where, when and what to study, though G12 students had more varied reasons, such as to aid concentration, find personal space, exercise time management, and manage stress. Students in both years remembered using library resources for assignments, but it was not a regular way of working for any student. Teacher encouragement varied, though there was a feeling that some teachers generally encouraged library use for studying purposes. G12 students identified possible evidence of library use through a requirement that bibliographies were compiled. However, students identified Internet use (by both students and teachers) and textbook provision as reasons why library use was not encouraged. G11 students did not identify subject areas where teachers had encouraged library use, but in G12 commonly identified subjects were English, history, and TOK. Students in both grades used library resources during the year, but the extent of that use, both in terms of frequency and variety of resources consulted, was varied. Lack of use of fiction resources in both year groups was marked. In G12, use of library resources was often in related to extended essay needs; students generally found potentially useful resources. All students used iBooks, mainly for word processing and Internet access; however, there was limited use of subscription databases. More G12 students accessed citation information on the library webpage, whereas only one G11 student did. This finding suggests that there is a greater need for citation information in the second year of the IBDP. Nearly all students used the library catalog successfully, though again the extent of use varied: in G12, students' remembered catalog use was focused on essay needs. Nevertheless, students in both years remembered asking librarians for help in finding materials whether located in the catalog or not. Both G11 and G12 students asked library staff to help find resources, with few instances of advice being sought regarding helpful materials, though more second-year IBDP students asked for advice and help in relation to citation needs.

Virtually all students considered time management to be the most useful attribute or skill that they developed during their IBDP experiences. For those students who linked various attributes or skills together, highlighted study and research skills and critical thinking was also mentioned as being of almost equal importance to time management. With greater experience, G12 students were able to discuss factors in more detail, with, for instance, not least a considerable appreciation for the need to manage time effectively.

G11 students mostly thought the library could help with core aspects, extended essay and TOK, and some for subject areas. G12 students had more detailed comments, again reflecting greater experience. A prime area for library support was the extended essay, though two students considered their choice of essay to be unusual, and this belief affected their perception about the potential of the library to help. Another major area of support, though to a slightly lesser extent, was the TOK essay. Students were divided about subjects; even those who thought the library could support subject studies mentioned some subjects for which library support was not relevant.

Importantly, student attitudes, behavior, and use of the library as a socialization zone changed when they were *required* to go to the library, rather than when it was a voluntary activity. This was a changed circumstance during the time the action research was in operation.

Therefore, interviews with these two different groups of students enabled the following common factors to be identified:

- Students had need and desire for quiet and space for a study environment.
- Time managements skills were most important to students.
- Students generally had used library resources for IBDP studies, as well as library services, such as the catalog, and ICT facilities in the library.
- Students use of library resources for IBDP focused on extended essay needs.
- Some, but not all, teachers used the library as part of IBDP assignment/classes.

- Students considered teachers and textbooks to be the most important sources of information for IBDP needs.
- Students considered that it was mainly English and history teachers who encouraged students to use the library.
- Students had asked the librarian for help to find resources.
- They considered that the library role in IBDP was mainly focused on the extended essay and TOK.

Did the Views of IBDP Students Change from the G11 Year to the G12 Year?

So the above findings showed some differences as well as similarities between two groups of students in G11 and G12. Did these findings change when the *same* group of students, who were interviewed in G11, finished their G12 year and completed the IBDP? What questions about student use emerged during the study?

These students still firmly saw the library as offering primarily "study space," where they could expect "silence" and be able to "do research." These were all words that students commonly associated with the library. In this way, several students thought positively about the library and felt they were motivated, both to come to the library and do things (i.e., study) while they were there. However, not all students thought that, and for one student, "the act of actually walking to the library to look for it [information] just sort of seems more hard." For this student, using the Internet was more convenient. As a study environment, students had preferences. For instance, they enjoyed using the library as a quiet place to aid concentration, especially as the final external diploma examinations approached. Comfort, home situation, and travelling (i.e., after school) were all factors for students in their choice of how and when they used the library for study purposes. Study time for students was associated with "study hall" periods, rather than other times of the day. Once in G12, these students were more aware of the need for and their exercise of time management skills, not least as it related to library use.

How did students research in G12? All students still used the Internet; at least one used it exclusively, but all used it daily, perhaps supplemented by other materials, including those from the library. Because wireless capability was in existence, students did not necessarily associate the provision and use of computers exclusively with the library. After all, they could use ICT anywhere in school. They were aware though that in G12 they were using the Internet more efficiently, both in terms of time and the skills and strategies they used in searching for things on the Internet. Several students' views of the library had changed while they had been on the program: one student commented that it was "completely different once you start the diploma and you appreciate how much [sic] resources you actually have in the library."

What did teacher encouragement look like to students? In practice it was found to be more of a general exhortation to use the library, rather than in relation to specific assignments. One student considered that library use "was more something you have to do individually, you're supposed to take that responsibility." Another student was surprised that it was only the English department that encouraged him to use the library, as he expected more "factual" based subjects to require student inquiry or research.

What did students perceive the main role and function of both the library and librarian to be in the IBDP? One student coined the use of the library as "an informative place to study." Others thought the main focus was as a place in which to do their research. Of the librarian's role, students thought that it focused on guidance and help with use of information and resources, though students thought that by G12 they were, and should be, independent in their use of the library, whereas "in 11th grade, we are completely lost," as one student said.

Did students think that the library was of personal value to them? One student thought that the library "gained more importance to me for studying" as she went through the program, as it gave her space for "my quiet, concentrated working," while another was generally happy with the library as she found it. A third student believed that "you can't go about it [IBDP] without a library 'cause that's really the place they [sic] need to be to do the studies." However, at the other extreme, another student considered it was not of value to him because of the Internet: "it's got everything now," he said succinctly.

Did students have sufficient ICT/Internet skills? Both teachers and, to a lesser extent, students noted that the latter's Internet-searching skills may be limited, but they generally improved during their IBDP years, due to practice and necessity (i.e., limited time). Nevertheless, students made extensive, daily use of the Internet for both school and other needs.

WHAT AN IBDP STUDENT'S LIBRARY USE LOOKS LIKE

The most important use of the school library for students in the study was as a place for studying. This was particularly so for study halls or "free periods" as students thought of it. For some students, they were required to be in the library for study hall. Being required to be in the library at a particular time threw up various issues to do with motivation, work ethic, behavior, and so on. (This was a school regulation that changed during the course of the research.)

Quantitative impact studies have all noted that the use of school libraries diminished as students progressed through high school (or studies did not include data for older students). However, this study suggests that the students used the library *differently*, not less.

Students did use library resources, though their use of the library may have been more occasional than the use of electronic resources (principally from the Internet). Nevertheless, the use of technology in the library was very strong.

Students had access to other sources of information, and these included subject departmental libraries and teachers' personal libraries. If this is a factor for some departments who, for various reasons, do not send students to research in the library, discrete collections can be relocated from the main library to subject departments, on the reasoning that that is where the students are.

On the other hand, the students in this study were limited in the amount of English language library and information facilities available to them, because they were in an international school in a country whose language was not English. For students in other contexts, a library infrastructure may exist, such as a national, state, or regional library system, and if it exists, it could be utilized by librarians for the benefit of students.

Students accessed the resources in various ways. The online catalog was not much used; students either learned where resources were or asked peers. They also looked around or asked the library staff to find things for them. The students had limited skills in locating resources, partly through little history of requiring such skills in previous school years. However, they needed this skill for the extended essay. Virtually everyone noted that the extended essay was perceived as the main support of the library to students and the IBDP, and it was a concern that this role could be overlooked.

Although students used technology, they rarely used databases, and usually only after encouragement and having been shown how they worked. As the literature found, students preferred the freedom of the Internet, rather than the structured basis of databases, even though some students were prepared to admit that some material on the Internet was not useful, relevant, or accurate. It was just easier to use and familiar, as the literature also found.

The Internet was a daily feature of students' lives, and they really could not think of life without it, therefore research that required means of information other than the Internet seemed unnatural and forced to students. However, some students were prepared to admit that they had limited Internet searching skills and they relied on features such as Wikipedia.

HOW THE STUDENTS PERCEIVED
THEIR SCHOOL LIBRARY

Perceptions are important as they allow values to be identified and expressed and could predict whether students would use the library. It was clear that how students perceived the school library changed during their IBDP candidature.

The library could be used as a social area by students, especially when students were required to be in the library (often due to limited facilities elsewhere in the school for them to use). Using the library as a social space added a social and emotional aspect to their perceptions. Some of this social use could manifest itself in behavior that is not normally considered appropriate in a library, such as using it as a student lounge. Such use could also be territorial too. When older students moved into areas or parts of the library, other students were sometimes not as willing to use the same area. It could also spoil what some students valued about the library—a quiet, calm environment. Therefore students could affect how the library was used and perceived by students of other ages. This perception also applied to teachers. Some were unwilling to send groups of students to the library during class time for research exercises, as they assumed that too many students would be there for study hall purposes, and could distract their students. Nevertheless, the image of the library as a quiet, book-dominated area contributed to its sense of uniqueness. At one extreme, this quiet image was used as part of a strategy to help relieve stress.

However, as students proceeded through the program, their views changed. They saw that the library had an information role as well as offering study space, which they could choose to use or not. Some second-year diploma candidates felt that there was a value and benefit in using the library as it helped them to use their time efficiently, complete required work, and prepare for examinations. Even those who did not value the library valued having a choice of venue and resources available to them. The library was also valued as being available to them throughout the school day. Many students arrived home too late and were too tired to study in the evenings, so they appreciated having opportunities to study during the school day, and this need to get work done at school may have assisted them with time management skills. It is worth remembering that as they progressed through G12, students experienced more pressure, and they found that work deadlines increased, not the least external deadlines. This could have been a new experience for them. They needed to review for external examinations, but they also had more freedom of time, and they needed to handle that time themselves.

DID USING THE LIBRARY BEFORE STARTING THE IBDP HELP STUDENTS?

The impact of students' library usage before entering the IBDP really depends on student mobility. If a student population is relatively stable, then the librarian will have time to influence how students use the library before they start IBDP. In a school, such as an international school, where students on average may only stay 18 months to 2 years, this is less practicable, but should be the aim. There are studies aiming to link or show benefits of undertaking the MYP, then the IBDP. Nevertheless, use of the library prior to starting the IBDP was felt to be a helpful factor by teachers who were involved in the study, and this also applied to bibliography education.

CONCLUSION

This is an account of how particular students used the library. The methodology, grounded theory, for the research does not claim to generalize. Indeed, even choosing different students in the same year at the same school could have produced varying findings. Any applicability of this research with other situations rests with the reader of the research. If you think these students are similar to those in your school and students you see in the library, and if the situations as described seem familiar, then that will affect your reflection on the research findings as presented in this book. It is the reflection that is important and an aim of this book. Now we have looked at one main group in a school's IBDP community (students), but we still need to look at the views and perceptions of others: teachers, administrators, and the librarian. As a result of the literature researched before the study and the information gathered during the study, school librarians may wish to apply the strategies given in the next section to their work.

PRACTICAL STRATEGIES FOR THE LIBRARIAN

- Be involved in developing school-wide study skills/information literacy policies prior to students starting the program and audit what skills are expected of students during IBDP. Do not forget the contexts of academic honesty and the IB learner profile.
- Plan or be involved in planning a seminar about study skills, as opposed to research skills, at the beginning of the IBDP, especially if your school library is involved in hosting regular study halls or periods for students. The timing

is important, as a well-timed seminar can assist in identifying expectations and ways of working. A seminar could form part of a wider induction to the program, but it does need to be held at the *beginning* of the program.

- Find out how time management skills are taught and reinforced during a student's IBDP candidature.

- Identify the/a role of the library in the program, not the least in discussions with the IBDP coordinator. It would be helpful to record decisions about the IBDP at the particular school and make them available in any school documentation for students, parents, and faculty.

- Liaise with faculty about how they see the library supporting IBDP students, which may well vary for different subjects.

- Liaise with academic and support IT facilities, so they are aware of the role of the library as it relates to the needs of IBDP students.

- Identify and use various Web 2.0 applications for library use and to help teachers make use of these resources in the classroom.

- Have discussions with the student council about how they see the library supporting the diploma students, especially vis-à-vis facilities for students, in particular those in G11 and G12. What do students have available for them in school for recreation and relaxation? It would be helpful to talk with the administration about this prior to liaising with students. An awareness of what student facilities exist may help the librarian decide how to run the library.

- Don't let the library be seen the only the place for study halls without an appreciation of what students do or need to do; and of who is going to supervise the students while they are in the library.

- Suggest that stress and relaxation classes be held for older students. Perhaps the librarian could hold a brain gym or similar sessions; these are techniques to promote greater well-being through gentle physical routines to stimulate brain efficiency. Brain gym is a particular technique for which it is possible to follow a certificated course as a trainer. There are other techniques, such as the Alexander Technique, that can be used. (A librarian could ask the school's drama teachers for more information about such techniques.)

7

---•◦•◦•---

TEACHERS, ADMINISTRATORS, AND THE LIBRARIAN IN THE IBDP

This chapter is concerned with the role of adults who are involved in the IBDP, specifically teachers, administrators, and librarians. The study that is the focus of this book researched the role of adults as well as students. This was to ascertain how adults perceived students and not only the way they studied but also their views of library support for the IBDP, which therefore could include support to relevant adults as well as students. A teacher from each of the six subject groups received an invitation to be interviewed; this was repeated in the second year of the action research. Other teachers were interviewed to cover core aspects of the program. The teachers, like students, came from a variety of countries to work in international schools, although they tended to come from a range of English-speaking countries, and thus could, broadly speaking, use a similar range of pedagogies.

In terms of their experience with school libraries, none of the teachers interviewed could remember anything about school library use being included in their teacher education programs. Teachers were specifically asked about education or awareness in "pedagogical *use* of a library." Most teachers interpreted the question to be about resource provision, although some also made connections with research and study. Lack of inclusion was also true of any subsequent professional development opportunities, including IB teacher workshops.

Some teachers had used the library as part of an assignment with IBDP students, though this was not a regular occurrence for these teachers. Of these, two had visited the library with their students, while another two had required students to research individually. Assessment varied, though two teachers mentioned the need to see students' bibliographies. One teacher specifically indicated a role for a librarian in assignments and liaised with the librarian in advance of the visit. Another teacher had developed his practice through working with librarians in each of the six international schools in which he had previously taught, and involved the librarian in planning for the internal assessment in his subject. However, several teachers considered their role was not to directly use the library space or the library collection but rather to encourage student use. Teachers assumed that students already knew how to use the library. Teachers perceived use of the library for students as providing a purposeful, serious place in which to study, in which use of library resources might be an added bonus.

Some teachers liaised with the librarian about new curriculum needs. For instance, one teacher noted that "whenever we teach a new novel, . . . we would let the librarian know we were teaching that book, and he was responsive." Departmental or personal libraries of books of teachers were also available to students. A factor for the existence of these collections included the distance between the school library and the subject departments. The library being far away from the classroom was given as a reason why it was not possible to use the school library in class time with their students. However, teachers also mentioned pressures of limited time in which to teach high-content courses; there was little or no time in which to encourage library use in class time.

While some teachers used the library for their own needs (generally English and history), teachers of other subjects did not generally see a library role in providing resources for their own teaching use. In some subject areas (e.g., sciences), textbooks provided sufficient resources while a group 5 teacher (mathematics) saw no role for the library, excepting a sole role in support of a mathematics extended essay.

Of the skills needed by students to succeed in the IBDP, most teachers thought time management skills were the most important. For some subjects, but not all, plagiarism was an issue, though only two teachers thought there was a role for a librarian in promoting academic honesty.

Teachers were asked to define the term *librarian*; there were varied responses. They were often unsure or inconclusive, although they tended to focus on resource management, the dissemination of information, and aspects of information literacy. Librarians were perceived as "educator[s] in how to go about understanding resources" and school staff members who have a role in "teacher training as well as student training" in the use of resources. One teacher specifically mentioned a role for a librarian as supervisor of study halls, reflecting that "where a librarian has to do it, it drives the librarian crazy, because they are having to do two jobs [including] having to be a disciplinarian."

Interviews with teachers in the following year focused on themes that were emerging from the research, namely skills falling under the broad heading of information literacy, plus student use of the Internet, a library role in the IBDP, and study periods (halls) and the library.

Teachers perceived that students needed a history of effective information handling skills and experience in using the library in their earlier school years. One teacher was surprised to reflect that diploma students required or perhaps expected to be given explicit instructions to do background research. She assumed that students would know this, as she had when she was a school student. Teachers thought that students needed to be able to use a variety of different resources at the same time; extrapolate information from several sources and create new information; understand how libraries were arranged; and be adept at bibliography construction, including citation in text. All teachers identified the need for students to have a heritage of library use and relevant information-based skills. The term *information literacy* was never used by the teachers.

One teacher noted a tension between the expectations of students identified in the IB learner profile, and a tradition of "spoon-feeding" students with information, a tradition that was typically associated with high-content courses. Teachers thought the ability to construct a bibliography was essential for all subject areas as well as the core requirements of the IBDP. Teachers' views about the utility of the library to support subject group needs varied with the subject, but there was broadly a divide between humanities and sciences. However library-friendly teachers were, they realized they were bound by limited time and high-content transfer courses. They had a view that education on information literacy–related issues should be pursued on a whole-school level, not just left to the librarian to develop. Teachers generally had concerns about student over-use of the Internet, and especially their inability to identify good or relevant sites and content. These concerns also related to student skills and critical thinking.

In terms of identifying a library role in the IBDP, teachers' views tended to focus on the extended essay, both for what was available physically in the library and the ability of the librarian in obtaining information and resources from elsewhere. Again a subject split was seen between the humanities/literature on the one hand and sciences/mathematics on the other; however, a role for the extended essay was noted by all teachers.

Teachers answered that they assumed students could use resources independently, but on reflection, they felt that this was, as one said, "a false assumption, but it's any easy one for teachers to make and allow themselves to make." So the assumption needed to be tested for and with students.

Teachers realized that students required a reason to visit the library, although when they perceived a use, there was a belief that students would value it. Nevertheless, teachers felt that if students were not required to be in the library for study halls or periods, they would not be motivated to visit it on their own, or that only more able students would do so. Teachers agreed that students would only value the library if "the teacher actually sees the library as a resource and uses it," as one teacher put it, thus modeling use for students.

Some teachers were concerned about the lack of documentation or reference to the role of the library in IBDP curricular literature. Others were unsure if such documentation referred to library use. They felt that it needed to be made explicit to validate the library role and encourage teachers to support and promote such a role.

They also saw a role for the library in supporting teachers with subject-based resources for IBDP. As one teacher commented "we're in the same boat as the students." Teachers made a distinction between their needs for subject teaching and more general professional development information, but especially relating to international education and pedagogy. As one remarked, "one thing I like is the library getting (and letting teachers know about) journal articles that basically keeps you up to date." Overall, teachers were influenced by their previous experience of libraries, whether as students themselves or earlier in their careers.

WHAT DID SENIOR ADMINISTRATORS THINK?

Two main senior administrators in the school in the study were separately interviewed in the second year of the study. They were asked to discuss themes that arose from the study in line with grounded theory principles.

Specific ongoing evaluation of the library vis-à-vis the IBDP was based in practice on "gut feeling" and observation. One administrator realized that the library "can't afford to be static . . . [but has] to respond to need, to numbers, to technology." Ideally, the library should support IBDP students in a dedicated manner, but in practice, other needs, other year groups, would also have a call on the library at the same time, as there was one library for the whole school (K–12).

The administrators considered that the most obvious role of the library in the IBDP was in relation to the extended essay but there was probably a hidden role of "indirect impact of the library and librarian with individual classrooms and individual subject groups of the diploma." As this was most likely undertaken on a one-to-one basis with individual teachers or departments, the only person who would have an overview of this would be the librarian.

Administrators had a strong feeling that librarians should model independent learning skills for both students and teachers, "the lead has to come from the librarian," which would set the tone for school expectations. In terms of inquiry and research, they noted that the lack of teacher experiences of research and the inquiry process, together with a reliance on textbooks in a high content–transfer teaching/learning environment, could limit the role of a library in the IBDP.

The administrators tended to agree with both teachers and students that time management and organizational skills were key factors to enable students to achieve the diploma, not the least average students succeeding in the diploma. This was in a school where the whole G11–G12 cohorts were IBDP candidates, and they had strong views that the diploma was a suitable curricula experience for all students.

Administrators, as would be expected, provided an overview of the school situation and were happy to talk in the abstract about libraries. As one said, it was refreshing to talk about a school service, without there being an agenda or issues attached. They were aware of cultural values associated with a library, and they noted psychological impact related to the image of a library. One noted that LIS impact research tried to influence the image of a library, although this administrator was skeptical of research that sought to identify causal links with student attainment, as it was, in practice, difficult to isolate variables to measure in educational matters. School libraries had therefore changed, and this was partly due to the efforts, views, and work of librarians. However, administrators considered that the "philosophies" needed to integrate the library within the school was an administrator's job, not a librarian's (albeit with the support and help of the librarian). Therefore it was an administration role to encourage teachers' use and promotion of the library in the school.

WHAT ARE THE QUESTIONS THAT ARISE FOR A LIBRARY IN A SCHOOL THAT OFFERS THE IBDP?

Let's look first of all at the issue of how a particular curriculum can affect a school library; how teachers taught and students learned affected how the school library was used. Students in the study experienced more lecture-style learning situations, with more content, especially during the second year of the IBDP, and relied more on textbooks. The need to cover content was a time pressure on teachers, and thus impinged on any potential use of the library in assignments.

Is transfer of content an issue in limiting library use? Kyburg, Hertberg-Davis, and Callahan (2007) identified lecture-style teaching format and time pressures in covering content in the IBDP, which Vanderbook (2006) found considerable. The focus of this pressure was final examinations (Stobie, 2007). This was not only the case with the IBDP as Williams and Wavell (2006) found in another curriculum, so it may be the case that content-transfer experiences are common for 16- to 18-year-old students, and, as a consequence of this type of teaching, library use by classes may be limited.

Does provision of textbooks affect library use? As course content-transfer vehicles, the provision and use of textbooks may affect library use and effectiveness. When provided for, textbooks were used extensively, especially in the first year of the course, and set expectations among students that this was the way to work and study, so that when they came to work on coursework and other requirements, they had limited experience of other ways of studying, and specifically for doing research. Students had faith in textbooks and observation of students in the school library showed that students mostly brought their own textbooks to work in study hall sessions in the library, and they tended not to use any other resources. When interviewed, students said that the most important sources of information for them were teachers and textbooks, a conclusion that is also reflected in a study by Latrobe and Havenar (1999), though it was not an IBDP study. Spreadbury and Spiller (1999) concluded that the provision and use of textbooks at schools in the United Kingdom had a negative impact on library use. Rafste (2003, 2005) found that students who used libraries as study space brought their own textbooks. Considering that these provided sufficient material to obtain good grades, students did not perceive the need for more information. It could be suggested that a content-rich transmitted curriculum environment, rather than one of constructivism, was prevalent in this study as it is in many schools worldwide. This issue of IBDP pedagogy was the reflection of a senior administrator in the study, who saw use of textbooks as appropriate in a non-constructivist curriculum and a useful resource for both teachers and students, although there should be a limit on the importance of such a resource.

Is the fact that the IBDP was a standard course for all G11–G12 students a factor on library use? Because there was a need to transmit significant amounts of content quickly, including to students who may be less able, then there may be implications for library use. The literature suggests that the IBDP is not suitable for academically weak students (McKenzie, 2001) nor all gifted learners (Kyburg et al., 2007). Nevertheless, some schools offered it as the standard course for all students (McCluskey, 2006; Rataj-Worsnop, 2003). Administrators who were interviewed in the study considered that the IBDP was achievable by most students, a view borne out by interviewed teachers, albeit with some concern about English as a second language (ESL) or English as an additional language students (EAL), and those who were considered less able. This concern, with implications for teaching styles and skill expectations and attainments, reflected (for mixed-ability students) a U.S. study that indicated a need for considerable scaffolding support by teachers (Burris, Welner, Wiley, & Murphy, 2007). Therefore, some students, who may be regarded as less able, may find it difficult to access or use libraries effectively.

What do teachers consider the main focus of library support for the IBDP? Although some teachers interviewed thought the library had a role in supporting IBDP subject groups, it depended on the subject. Any library role was considered limited in groups 2 and 4 (languages and sciences, respectively), and teachers could not perceive of a relevant role in group 5 (Mathematics) subjects. Overall, most teachers who were interviewed thought any library role really related to both the extended essay and the TOK essay. If the extended essay is the focus for the school library program, it is, in a wider context, important to identify the extent of student choice of diploma as opposed to certificate options, that is, if the certificate option is more prevalent, those students do not need to complete extended and TOK essays, so library support may not be relevant to or needed by such students.

The study found that teachers used the library both directly and indirectly, as some teachers saw their role as not directly using library resources with students but rather by encouraging library use by individual students.

Do teachers use library and librarian support to complete assignments? This is the most direct use (i.e., a teacher with a specific aim in mind visits the library with a class). Students remembered occasional use of this strategy during their IBDP candidature though teachers interviewed indicated that some had incorporated the library into assignments, some fairly regularly, at least initially in the two-year course (before pressures of time built up), but others irregularly, and one teacher, once only. In Norway, a study by Rafste (2003), which included one IBDP school in the study, found that teachers did not perceive it to be their role to include library use in their teaching styles, nor was there any indication that they encouraged library use by students.

How can teachers encourage students to use the library? Twelfth-grade students in the study remembered that only the English Department encouraged library use. This is similar to an impact study by Hay (2005, 2006) in Australia, where a similar scenario was found. Such reduction in encouragement as students progressed to higher grades was consistent with other studies (McLelland & Crawford, 2004; Spreadbury & Spiller, 1999), though subject teacher encouragement of use corresponded with student subject use. Most teachers in these studies never referred their students to the library, though the reason why was not clear. However, one student in the present study thought that teachers assumed students would use the library without being advised, a view which also came through teacher interviews. Streatfield and Markless (1994) found school libraries in the United Kingdom were more effective if they reflected pedagogies of individual teachers within a school, rather than try to develop a model of library provision predicated on one desired pedagogy, especially if it only reflected an LIS paradigm. The present study found that teachers worked in different ways, not the least reflecting their subject specialties. One effect of lack of encouragement of library use by teachers in general might be seen in a clear trend of declining library use by grade 10, which was identified in U.S. impact studies (Callison, 2005). The teachers in the present study showed support for the library in general, and it is probable they assumed students had the skills to use the library, irrespective of their academic and ICT skills levels. However, when teachers reflected during interviews, they had some understanding that students' varying abilities could result in some students, but not all, being able to effectively use the library without prompting. Teachers in this study matched the findings of Todd and Kuhlthau (2005b) where teachers in Ohio had positive views about the library when they were asked to think about it; although, generally speaking, teachers saw the relationship as being between students and the librarian, and not between themselves and the librarian.

Do teachers use the library directly or individually, and if so, can they be seen as role models of library use? Teachers can and do, of course, use the library for their own information and interest, but Boekhorst and van Veen (2001) found that while most school libraries in the Netherlands provided resources for teachers, their use of these resources was limited. In the present study, the ability of the library to provide resources for teachers of IBDP subjects was only perceived as being useful by teachers of groups 1, 3, and 6. Some thought that the resources of interest to them could/would also be used by students. So, there was a somewhat limited view of the library role in this regard, though it differed from supporting teachers' professional needs (e.g., on pedagogy and educational research/trends, especially a library service alerting them to new items). This service was seen as valuable, and reflects a study by Williams (2006), who recommended that librarians should promote such a role or service. An observation exercise of teacher use of the library in the study indicated that teachers also used the library for their own recreational and personal needs, and by doing so, modeled library use for students.

Are teachers educated in the use of libraries as a teaching strategy, and where does their experience of school libraries come from? In interviews, teachers could remember no input in initial teacher training programs or ongoing professional development (e.g., workshops provided by the IBO) that looked at pedagogical use of a school library to provide strategies on how to incorporate the school library into their teaching styles. They therefore had limited awareness of skills students needed to use school libraries effectively. One teacher had worked with six librarians in six international schools, but for most teachers, their library experiences were gained either as school students themselves or as students in tertiary education. Olen's (1995) study of trainee teachers in South Africa suggested that due to limited use of the library as school students themselves, they would not have a model or expectations of a school library on which to base pedagogical practice. Asselin (2005) found little input about school libraries in pre-service teacher education courses in Canada, while others identified a need to raise awareness of information literacy in teacher training courses in Europe (Merchant & Hepworth, 2002; Rafste, 2005). However, Williams and Wavell (2006) concluded that while information literacy as a term was commonly used in the LIS, it was not naturally used in mainstream education, and was predicated on a constructivist approach to learning, which may not be a prevalent form of pedagogy in a particular school. Indeed, a span of pedagogies, as Streatfield and Markless (1994) identified, may exist in a particular school at any one time.

How can school staff evaluate their library in relation to the IBDP? In the study, this was mainly through informal, ongoing observation and "gut feeling", especially by administrators (as a study of principals in New York by Everhart [2006] also found), and not specifically related to the needs of the IBDP. Teachers had made no formal evaluation; their perception of the library was mostly determined by their subject specialties, and any use or value of the library was predicated on that. No reference in IBDP *subject documentation* prompted any teacher evaluation of library use. Interestingly, prior to the interview, one administrator was given a piece of impact research to read, a study that found causal links between student achievement and the school library. He thought it was interesting, but was not convinced by the findings. He considered that there were many contributory factors on student achievement that could include the school library. This administrator considered that the report would be most likely read only by the school library community. Impact study researchers have noted the need to promote a body of research among administrators (Callison, 2005); indeed Pratt (1994) and Montiel-Overall (2005) observed little synergy between mainstream educational literature and that of school librarianship.

What could be the library impact on teachers? While impact studies have mostly focused on student achievement, Farmer (2006) concluded that a library may have more impact on teachers than students. In this study, a number of teachers used the library for a variety of reasons, which differed from a U.S. study by KRC Research (2003). In the KRC Research study, teachers, although stating the library's value for students, rarely used libraries themselves. While they had a belief structure, it did not extend to modeling such a belief. Still, observation and interview in the IBDP study can only uncover so much. Overall, as a library, it was as a place in which to work and from which to borrow resources, that had the most obvious impact on teachers, otherwise impact may be indirect or hidden.

WHAT ABOUT THE LIBRARIAN?

Using memo technique in grounded theory, a librarian's perspective was briefly developed for the research. Otherwise, in practitioner research, where the librarian was the practitioner, it would be difficult to provide such a narrative. In memo technique using semi-structured questions, the librarian wrote responses in a particular time frame (30 minutes) and they were not altered after that time, so it is as near to spontaneity as possible. The following snapshot of the librarian's written concerns show that they reflected and mostly supported findings from students, teachers, and administrators:

1. Supervision of study halls was a significant job activity on a daily basis.
2. Use of ICT in the library had low-grade use.
3. Subject departments overall made limited use of the library, though there were exceptions.
4. Provision of textbooks affected the library.
5. Reference to a school library and librarian is not available in IBDP *subject* documentation.
6. Some cooperation and liaison between teachers and librarian existed.
7. Information services to teachers were prioritized, with some evidence that they were valued.
8. Extended essay role was a major aspect of the role of the library and librarian in the IBDP.
9. Support was available for core features, when the librarian was a TOK teacher and supervised CAS activities/projects in the library.
10. Use of technology was important as a major way of communicating and projecting the image of the library and librarian amongst teachers as much if not more than with students.

In the absence of research about the role of the librarian in the program, how did the IBDP community in the present study view the librarian? What did they perceive the librarian's role in the IBDP to be?

Teachers were mostly inconclusive when asked to define a school librarian, though several made links to resource provision and information expertise, and this partly reflected their experiences of librarians (as Williams (2006) also found). It is worth noting that the teachers' experience of librarians included memories of librarians they knew while they were school and university students themselves and not only as practicing teachers. Indeed, students had fairly stereotypical views, which reflected KRC Research (2003). No respondent in the study identified a specific qualification or professional background or status of a librarian, but teachers articulated individual characteristics and qualities that were appropriate for a fellow faculty member. Therefore, it may be that personal qualities, matched to pedagogies that faculty employed, are more relevant than a precise qualification or experience base. What a librarian is called and how that person is educated varies from country to country, and for an international curriculum, these are issues that need to be borne in mind, because one (national) system cannot be adopted for IB purposes. Turner (2007) found "no definitive model for how a school library should be staffed, despite the recommendations of professional organizations" (p. 12). Indeed, Oberg (1995) and Roys and Brown (2004) found it was personality characteristics that enabled teacher-librarians to be effective; these attributes include a positive attitude and pro-active stance (Henri & Boyd, 2002).

Many students and teachers firmly saw a main role of the librarian as provider of help and assistance to locate and identify resources, both those in the library collection, and electronically. For all teachers, they believed this role to be mainly focused on the extended essay requirement. Another de facto role was behavior manager as supervisor of students during their study halls, which took place in the library.

The study found that liaison and cooperation with subject faculty, rather than true collaboration, existed. This disagrees with some of the literature about school libraries. The professional literature about collaboration is extensive, but what exactly is collaboration? The literature is based largely on a belief that a strong collaborative structure needs to be in place in a school in order for students to develop adequate skills and fully benefit from library interaction in the curriculum. However, whether teachers have accepted the concept has not been identified (Todd & Kuhlthau, 2005b). Todd, in an interview from evidence-based practice research, suggested that collaboration rarely existed, suspected that teachers did not see it as a part of their role, and noted that the concept of collaboration brought considerable pressure on school librarians from within the profession (Kenney, 2006). Montiel-Overall (2008) identified several levels of interaction with teachers ranging from communication to cooperation and finally collaboration. She found some examples of collaboration at the elementary level, but none at the high school level.

CONCLUSION

The study therefore generated the following grounded theory:

> The impact of a school library on the IBDP depended on several factors. The influence of teachers was important, and their awareness and enthusiasm for school libraries and encouraging their students to use such facilities was vital. Often, teachers' perceptions and values of school libraries were significantly influenced by their previous experiences, including those as school students. Teachers did not become aware of the utility of school libraries through initial or in-service teacher education programs, nor was it highlighted in IBDP curricular literature, therefore the onus was on individual teachers. Students used libraries, often as directed by teachers and/or accepted the values associated with school libraries by teachers. The use of textbooks was a strong deterrent to potential use of school libraries as relevant resources of information. Students used school libraries primarily as a place of study. The librarian in the study tried to relate the school library to various perceptions and values of individual teachers and students, rather than the advocated roles in a library and information sector paradigm. The most articulated and perceived use of the school library was in relation to the extended essay.

PRACTICAL STRATEGIES FOR THE LIBRARIAN

- Think about the role of the school principal and other administrators in relation to the school library.
- Consider the library needs of faculty, both in terms of their subject and professional development.
- Undertake a short observation exercise of your library to see how it is used.
- Develop either a formal or informal research exercise in your library, involving interviewing selected students and staff.
- Consider pedagogical use patterns by subject faculty in your school.
- If you are going to be in an IBDP school, reflect on your own priorities. What do you perceive to be your role? What are the tensions and opportunities involved in attaining your aims?

8

A CONSUMER-FOCUSED SCHOOL LIBRARY

This chapter focuses on how the school library may be used *by* teachers and students. The library is more than a static facility because the librarian makes the library a dynamic place where the available services provide a necessary contribution to the school's IBDP community.

USES OF THE LIBRARY AND THE LIBRARIAN

When looking at how the library may be used, it would be helpful to brainstorm the sorts of uses that could be made of a library in support of a curriculum that has an inquiry-centered ethos and in which learner qualities and skills are being developed. In such a scenario, perhaps a school librarian would enable some of the following to occur:

- The library would be a welcoming, relaxing environment that supports a learner in growing confidence and motivation.
- The library should be a dedicated, named facility that is accessible by students throughout and beyond the formal school day.
- The library should provide information in a variety of formats, such as print, digital, audio and visual, at various levels of ability ranges.
- The IBDP would enable learning opportunities, which are supported by the librarian and others. These would be opportunities for the students to exercise choice, judgment, and responsibility in selecting reading material that may interest them; be responsible for managing their choices of activities in the library; and develop judgment in assessing the utility of information for their particular needs.
- The librarian provides spaces for class and individual use.
- The librarian creates space for small groups to research, read, write, discuss, and evaluate.

- The librarian selects materials for an up-to-date collection that not only reflects and values cultures of students at the school but also opens students' minds to other cultures, ways of life, and values.

- The collection shows a value for a school community's mother tongues or home languages through representative collections of reading and language material in individual languages and dual-language texts in the library.

- The librarian develops an environment where students can seek out answers to their questions and reflect on what they learn. Typically, this is felt to be optimized and valued through a quiet, calm atmosphere, though the space does not necessarily need to be quiet to be useful to the students.

Developing a library to be used in these ways will involve working more with teachers in their pedagogical use of a school library. This will, in turn, create more opportunities to work with students.

WHAT IS PEDAGOGICAL USE OF A SCHOOL LIBRARY?

The notion of pedagogical use of the school library has been mentioned in the previous chapters in relation to questions that teachers were asked as part of the IBDP library research project. What is pedagogical use, and how can teachers achieve it?

Probably everyone thinks they know what a school library is for; it is usually seen as a "good thing," a desirable and pleasant place in a school, but there is usually little articulation of what the school library means *to a teacher*. For instance, use of the library was not taught as a pedagogical tool in initial teacher education or in-service training, such as IB workshops. This lack of suggestions for use of the library applies to IBDP curricular information whose main readership are teachers. If there have been no references to the school library in educational training opportunities, the views of teachers are based on their own experiences in using school libraries. This would mean they were drawing on experiences when they were school students themselves, and they may have had very poor school libraries. Even if they did experience some library service, it may not reflect recent practice.

Teachers and librarians should work together on designing assignments for students in IB programs. By doing so, this values the skills, knowledge, and perspectives of adults involved in the learning process, as recommended in the supporting text found in the IB *Learner Profile* document. Here is a list of suggestions for librarians to help encourage collaboration between themselves and teachers:

- Communicate. Talk with teachers about how the teaching and learning situation would be helped by working together rather than just asking for a list of resources. To get the most out of the experience, the operative word is *talk*. A dialog needs to take place. At the beginning, it doesn't need to be lengthy or involved. Most communication in schools tends to take place in short periods of time, perhaps on the way to somewhere else! It is better to communicate regularly, even if only in brief, rather than try to schedule a more lengthy meeting at the outset.

- Purchase new materials when needed. Specific projects may require the purchase of new materials. Because librarians are trained to think about resources flexibly, you may be able to suggest use of existing items in the library collection or in other parts of the school, as well as materials that may be available commercially and/or online.

- Know that students need and develop skills in using text and information over time. As with any other learning situation, this will not just happen in a library setting, but will involve planning, discussion, and respect for the process.
- Recognize that expectations set up through an assignment or activity are unlikely to happen if there is little or no follow-through, that is, the librarian should check with the teacher if the library has the right resources to answer the assignment/project, in appropriate quantities and at the right level(s).
- Model the role of an information seeker. Although the main focus of the library collection will be for young people, there may be sections, such as a staff or professional development collection, that are devoted to the needs of adults, staff, and parents in the school community. Other library materials such as periodicals, newspapers, databases, and some text material could be used by adults as well as by students. By modeling library use for students, you, the teachers, and other adults provide a valuable role model for the concept of lifelong learning and aspects of the IB *Learner Profile*.

HOW TO DEVELOP PEDAGOGICAL USE OF THE LIBRARY

One way to initiate the development of the pedagogical use of the library is to allow faculty to talk about their library usage. See if you can find out the reasons why teachers may not use the library with their students. If they tell you they have no time, do not see it as their role, or do not perceive how to use the library as a teaching and learning tool, you will know the challenge ahead of you. Raising this issue at a school forum such as a general faculty meeting or professional development occasion (or if you want to begin with a smaller audience, a subject faculty meeting) allows faculty to let you know their needs and indicates your interest in working with them to make changes in their use of the library. In a short but focused way, ask colleagues some of the following questions, and see the discussion flow.

1. What pedagogical use of the school library do colleagues remember from their initial teacher education and/or in-service professional development opportunities they have attended? (These questions can also be asked in a survey format.)
2. How could members of faculty use the library in their own teaching practices and styles?
3. What were/are the advantages of doing so?
4. What were/are the drawbacks?
5. How could this benefit the students?

Such a discussion allows participants to focus on their experiences, ideas, and concerns. It will also help you learn how the faculty views the library, and, hopefully, some good practice may result in terms of practical steps towards increased library usage or awareness of possible contributions.

Should this result in any professional development, you should be prepared to offer introductions to different databases in the library, any specific collections you have to support teaching, and any teaching about creating bibliographies or helping control plagiarism.

A LIBRARY ENVIRONMENT

An optimum library environment could enable elements of the qualities and skills identified in the IB *Learner Profile* to be practiced and developed, and with regard to requirements of academic honesty. This includes identifying resources available to students and teachers. Providing bibliographies of available materials can be helpful when annotated with information about the content and level of information. A list of popular magazines available in the library as well as URLs to any databases of periodical information should be available on a bookmark, handout or electronic information for teachers and students.

Other "resources" include equipment such as digital cameras, together with recording and reproduction facilities. Sometimes the library can be used to "present" a culminating event from the classroom. The real focus of the library staff is to provide a positive environment where discovery, inquiry, and learning may take place, and where students are empowered through the experience of learning how to manage information in their classrooms. The library can give them the confidence to manage their own information needs.

If available resources are to be used and used wisely, what librarians refer to as "information literacy" is important and useful. While mere location and mechanical skills are important and probably more visible, the more abstract skills of critical thinking and analysis are more important. It is a challenge for the school librarian to change the perceptions of faculty, students, and others, concerning the benefits that come from students engaging in these skills in the library setting.

PRACTICAL STRATEGIES FOR THE LIBRARIAN

- Engage administrators, teachers, and parents to come to the library to help model the use of information found there.

- Develop a library policy or mission statement. This should identify the expectations for users of the library. This statement should be included in mainstream school documents such as staff handbooks, and included with other school-wide policies as well as in curriculum documents.

- Consider the name given to the library in your institution in relation to effective communication and the benefit of having a clear image with the library's customers. Does the name use a phrase that may or may not include the word "library" (e.g., resource center, school library media resource center, learning resource center, etc.)? Is this phrase reduced to an acronym, the meaning of which, through repeated use, becomes further obscured? Consider how widely this phrase is understandable to students whose mother tongue is not English. What is the word for library in their language? Other terms instead of the word library are used for various reasons—not least to be more current, hip, or trendy—but are these terms meaningful to members of the school community? What do people in the school call the library on a daily basis? Is it different than its formal name?

- Consider where are the library facilities located on campus. Is it centrally situated or easily accessible for the school population? Could it be moved if a better location was available? Is it suitable for the purposes the school administrators and teachers have decided they want for the library? Is the library location effectively guided or signed throughout the school campus? Is the library referred to in school documentation, and is information about library facilities and services easily found on the school website?

- Consider whether the school library have its own easily found webpage that is kept up-to-date, is interesting, and links students to resources throughout the world.

- Consider the hours of the school library. When is the school library available to its customers? Is it open for students and staff throughout and beyond the formal school day?

- Consider how the library is staffed. Does the school employ someone who is qualified and experienced in children's and young adult literature and the information and research needs of students of all levels and all ages? Is that person employed full time? Are there support staff and/or technicians? What are the job titles of the library staff? Do they accurately describe what they do?

- Consider how library development and improvement in the school is achieved. Is there a committee with school-wide membership, chaired by a senior administrator to concern itself with "the big picture"?

- If no library "Advisory Committee" exists, consider who evaluates the way the library is used. Is this done systematically?

- Consider how formal communication concerning the library achieved in school. For instance, is it achieved through staff, faculty, and/or departmental meeting structures?

And these suggestions are for the IB itself (through members of faculty who are involved as workshop trainers or who assist with work groups to revise subject documentation):

- IBDP subject and core workshop trainers should include as an intrinsic element of workshops the importance of the *use* of the library as an inquiry-friendly environment. Trainers should emphasize the importance of promoting library use as useful pedagogical practice for teachers of the IBDP. Unless library use is clearly articulated, outdated views may predominate.

- Statements about library *use* should be made in IB *curriculum* documentation. This is because teachers look at such documentation regularly, rather than documentation about applying to be an IB school (and where information about the library tends to only appear).

9

ROLES OF THE IBDP
LIBRARY AND LIBRARIAN

Initially, librarians often want to know what the IB requires of a library in a school that wants to offer the IBDP. However, IB-sponsored guidelines or specific library standards do not exist. This sometimes comes as a surprise, not least to librarians.

ARE ROLE STATEMENTS ABOUT SCHOOL
LIBRARIES AND THE IBDP NEEDED?

Because IB library guidelines do not exist, this question is asked from time to time. The lack of guidelines is notable especially when one considers that statements about the function and provision of school libraries are documents that the LIS in various countries, and indeed internationally, have been familiar with for a number of years. So why do IBDP school librarians feel the need for role statements about school libraries?

Such documents, often produced by professional organizations in the LIS world (with a few exceptions, such as Canada and New Zealand, where they are produced by government agencies), now tend to focus more on curriculum (Todd, 2003). They have also linked libraries to ICT and information literacy as well as use of space and resources, such as in Australia (Australian School Library Association, 2006) and in the United Kingdom (Barrett & Douglas, 2004); and naturally everyone will be familiar with the *Standards for the 21st Century Learner* (American Association of School Librarians, 2007, 2009).

Generally, standards were traditionally associated with input measures, whereas a newer trend is to relate standards to both learning process and outcomes. However, there is some concern that an exact definition of a school library needed to be firmly articulated before standards can be really effective (Williams, Wavell, & Coles, 2001). Indeed, Wavell (2004) noted that both guidelines and standards were developed during an environment of accountability, where the need for effectiveness needed to be demonstrated, and it may be that the plethora of documents may result in "confusion and frustration" for individual practitioners (p. 13).

That statements about school libraries were developed mostly by professional LIS organizations suggests that there is or was little synergy between professional and research literatures of education and school librarians, as Montiel-Overall (2005) pointed out in a North American context. Pratt (1994) went further and noted little mention of school libraries in curricular documents; there is a question about the role adopted by LIS organizations, which may more properly belong to statutory bodies (Everhart, 2000).

Nevertheless, school librarians and their professional organizations clearly believe in the need for statements about school libraries, even if they are non-binding. Statements are based on a premise of benefit of use from provision, and, importantly, may *assume* a need for resource-based learning approaches and information literacy, sometimes *without* a statement or understanding of underpinning constructivist approaches to learning. The school library sector has focused and relied upon guidelines as a means of promoting the future of school libraries. Organizations have developed considerable energy on producing guidelines, whose readership may be mostly within the LIS world. Sadly, those involved with school libraries may be frustrated or not understand why there may be an overall low profile (or understanding) of school libraries in the general educational landscape. As a result, librarians may have unrealistic expectations about the power or influence of guidelines, which may, conversely, be mostly marketed within the profession or specialty, rather than to allied professions, and may moreover promote ideal situations.

So how can the real world be identified in terms of school libraries, and how, when advocating the use of guidelines, can a librarian counter a typical comment from administration: "Show me evidence about how the school library works in the real world—what is its contribution?"

Where is the research about impact or use of a school library in the IBDP? In terms of published research, there really isn't a research base apart from Latuputty (2005) and the present study, which are both practitioner based, which is no bad thing. There is a need both for accounts of library contributions to be written (perhaps published by the developing commercial publication department of the IB) and for accounts of library research and practice to be included in journals, conferences, and other places where teachers and administrators naturally look for their professional development, rather than journals in the school library sector.

So, despite there being no officially endorsed role statements to tell us what an IB library is supposed to look like, we can still determine what the role of an IB library looks like in practice. Through the present writer's study, we have examined separately various groups of students and faculty in relation to their experiences of the IBDP and the school library. Let's put them together to see what an IB school library looked like to them.

NARRATIVE OF ONE IBDP SCHOOL COMMUNITY'S RELATIONSHIP WITH THEIR SCHOOL LIBRARY AND LIBRARIAN

Teachers at the school may have had experience of another international school and/or schools in national systems, most probably in schools in an English-speaking country in which they were born and educated. The secondary school they attended as students may not have had a developed library nor anyone to manage it. It may have been called a library, but its main function would have been as a study area for older students. At university, a library may have been used as a place of study, with some research involved. Initial teacher education courses attended would not include use of the library, that is, as a facility that teachers could use pedagogically. As teachers rarely referred to libraries in previous international or other schools they worked in, they may not have experienced "good practice" (from an LIS perspective). For IBDP teachers at the international school, there was pressure on available teaching time due to the need to cover considerable content. As teachers came from different countries, pedagogical practice varied, often with an individual teacher.

Some subject teachers used the library as individuals. They borrowed resources for teaching purposes, though this varied between subjects (and could depend on the existence of departmental and/or personal libraries). Some used the library for subject-specific periodicals (including titles of a professional development nature); borrowed subject-based resources and other resources for personal or recreational use; or used a personal laptop computer and marked student work in the library. However, teachers tended not to take students to the library, though occasionally, in class, teachers encouraged their students to use library resources for their coursework. Some specifically requested students to ask the librarian about queries concerning citation and bibliography.

Students included those who moved from country to country, some with previous experience of international schools. Students may also be abroad for the first time, so they have had prior experience of a national system. English may not be the mother tongue of all students. Their previous library experience will be varied, and it may be that overall their library experience and information skill development is limited.

At the beginning of the IBDP program, students were informed they had individual study periods (called study halls), rather than lessons with teachers, that they were required to spend in the library. Students invariably completed homework in the library, bringing textbooks and everything needed with them. G11 students had little experience of using a library; were unsure of where things were and how to find things; tended not to ask for help; and relied on textbooks. As they generally received good grades, they saw little relevance or benefit in reading wider than textbooks. Completing homework tasks was standard for G11 students, though in G12, students completed coursework for subjects and undertook an individual extended essay. Some students used the library for research for this essay, and asked the librarian about citation and referencing conventions. All students used the Internet for information. Towards the end of G12, students began to review for final examinations; some used the library to secure a quiet environment in which to do so. Some experienced pressure, and nearly all found that time management skills were most important to their success.

Pressure on space in the school—and the library—arose in part as students did not have a student lounge or common room. The only place they could go to on a regular basis, when they were not taught, was the library. The only partial exception was the canteen, though some teachers—and students—had reservations about this being an appropriate venue for study halls. A regulation change in 2006 meant that G11 students could not use the canteen for study hall. This put pressure on the library to accommodate a larger number of older students. Appropriate behavior (as defined by adults and some students) deteriorated as students did not perceive the function of the library and used it as a lounge. Teachers perceived that the library was mainly used for study hall, peopled by larger numbers of students, and were reluctant to allow other students (or bring groups) to the library for research.

Nevertheless, some students used the library for information, though all students used the Internet. Some students used databases, for which subscriptions were made through the library budget, and which the librarian promoted. Few students used the library catalog. Most students borrowed library resources infrequently, with the exception of laptop computers that were used daily.

The library was staffed throughout and beyond the formal school day. There was a professional librarian, who encouraged library use, liaised with teachers about development of the library collection in support of various IBDP subject needs, and informed staff of library additions and developments. The librarian was also the only supervisor of IBDP students in the library and may have been perceived as representing authority and enforcing rules. Few students asked library staff for help, though when it happened, it was usually to help them find information and resources in the library. The librarian may have been influenced by LIS secondary literature that promoted collaboration, which was focused on information literacy as a major activity of the librarian. However, this did not reflect reality.

Perceptions of members of the IBDP school community groups, who were involved in the research, could determine how the library was used. Teachers, administrators, and students all felt that the main focus of possible library use was the extended essay. In terms of value and evaluation, the library was highly regarded by both administrators and faculty as being a useful facility, but little specific evaluation (related to IBDP needs) was evident. A focus on the role and expectations of a library are not identified in IBO/IBDP literature, but explicit IBDP documentation of the role of the library could focus thinking and expectations of faculty. While brief reference was made to library support in extended essay documentation, there was little or no reference to library use in IBDP curricular documentation, which was the only place subject teachers would normally look.

In the absence of any specific DP curricular or pedagogical encouragement that teachers should use a library, curricular use in fact varied between individual teachers, possibly according to their own education and previous experience of libraries. There was little or no pedagogical underpinning of library use; little concrete encouragement to use the library for ongoing needs was given to students. Teachers saw the library in a limited manner (as far as LIS-advocated models of school libraries are concerned), thus the librarian seemed to aim for a school library model that was not in line with the expectations or practices of prevailing pedagogies within the school

Those involved in this study (who were interviewed) reflected on their use of libraries—something that was unusual for them. One student did not value the library, suggesting that it was irrelevant as information needs could be totally met by use of the Internet and textbooks. Most students and some teachers who were interviewed were satisfied with library provision and their use of it. Some students felt they were helped by library service, and they valued the help. Some teachers felt that this was the case, though more teachers had views about how the library could be improved and be more relevant to the IBDP, at least as far as study halls were concerned. Some teachers saw no role for the library as far as their subjects were concerned. All teachers, administrators, and most students, however, thought that a library impacted (or could impact) the extended essay. This was the most often and commonly mentioned element of the IBDP in relation to the school library.

Although this narrative brings together the collective perspectives of a community, for a school library and its librarian, it is not a comprehensive picture. Unlike students, who naturally focus on their own concerns, and possibly teachers, who will typically focus on their subject and the age ranges of students they may teach, one librarian may well support the needs of a whole school, not just grades 11–12. In an international school, the needs of the whole school may encompass "K–12", a very wide age range. What the library and the librarian did in relation to IBDP needs was extrapolated from the general working day of a school library, and, in reality, various functions of both library and librarian would have occurred simultaneously. Neither the library nor the librarian catered exclusively to the needs of IBDP. Rather the library served the needs of the continuum of students, and their teachers, within an age range of 3 to 18 years.

Do present readers resonate with this account? Are there perhaps some similarities? Are there perhaps considerable differences from a reader's own library and experiences? It was what one IB library looked like to particular students, teachers, administrators, and a librarian—but what did that library look like to the IB itself? As mentioned earlier in the book, there have been limited statements by the IB about library provision and, more importantly, use of the library and its librarian. But there are a few references—from the archives, as it were—that may still be relevant today. These are isolated sources but they illustrate tensions and possibilities that relate to the possibly underdeveloped (or, rather, unarticulated) role of school libraries in support of the IBDP.

We have already referred to a speech by a librarian to a conference of principals in the IBEAM region in 1995 (Clark, 1995) that was reproduced in an issue of *IB World*: the theme of the speech was that the library was underused in the IBPD, but full of potential.

Not long after that, there was a meeting held at IBCA, in 1997, of the then-named Committee of Librarians of IBO Schools. The report of the meeting indicated that the limited role of librarians in curriculum development was discussed. While there was a growing awareness of research skills and the concept of independent learning and an awareness of the growing role of librarians as "facilitators in the teaching and learning process," no specific action was taken to further this role, though further thought should be given to such a role. Furthermore, a librarian should be involved in development planning. The IBO was keen to support such a role, but such cooperation was considered to be a matter for schools themselves, and not something the IBO could "mandate"; however, "the quality of such co-operation between librarians, teachers and school management might be commented upon in the course of authorization and evaluation visits to schools offering IB programmes" (Committee of Librarians of IBO Schools, 1997, p. 4). This really suggests that it is the authorization and evaluation visits that are key to generating change in schools.

Shortly prior to this, in an issue of the magazine *IB World*, a librarian articulated what he considered the role of an IB library to be. This was a time when there was only one IB program in existence—the diploma. Cordoba (1994) identified the role and benefit of using the school library in support of the IBDP, positing that the school library is a significant socioeconomic and educational resource in an information society. Furthermore, he argued that adult role models are important, as they help students to use the library. He imagined a scenario where students together with their teachers both engaged in the same purpose: "consulting, researching, reading." It is the research or inquiry process that really focused Cordoba's attention, as he said that "the IB library is also a research library and will be organized to reflect the stages of research from the preliminary search for materials to the critical analysis and use of those materials" (Cordoba, 1994, p. 36).

So, we have looked at a perceived need for library guidelines in order to identify a role or roles for the school library and the librarian. We have also looked at a study that showed what one IB library looked like and the lived experience of some of its users. Then we looked at some sources "from the archives" that suggest both tensions and potential for growth associated with a library and librarian role in an IB context.

However, rather than isolating the library out of DP requirements, which is what a separate role statement would do, the library may be seen as more integral and holistic to the program if the librarian related her/himself and the library facility to the *Programme Standards and Practices for the Diploma* in general, which is what other areas of the school are required to do. While this is at the price of clarity that could result from considered, articulated statements about school libraries, it is also the case that subject teachers would not necessarily be part of an IB standards reconciliation process, as it would perhaps occur more naturally between the librarian and administrators, though school responses and contributions to standards should be communicated in the school. For subject teachers, the documentation they would generally and regularly refer to would be diploma subject syllabi. Ideally it would be helpful if a statement about the role of the library, however brief, would be written into such documents. Nevertheless, it is to the program standards that we need to look at next to see if it is possible to identify what role(s) can be identified for an IBDP library and its librarian.

IB PROGRAMME STANDARDS AND PRACTICES

These standards are common to all IB programs and relate to all aspects of school life. The new document, which was made available in the fall of 2010, became effective from the beginning of 2011 and replaced a standards document dated 2005 (it is vital that librarians refer to the latest version on the OCC). The current seven standards are grouped under three broad headings: philosophy, organization, and curriculum. The latter two are then further subdivided into generic headings such as leadership, resources, collaborative planning and teaching and learning. Practices are seen as further refinements of individual standards. The arrangement of the document is that standards are listed as applying to all programs (as they were in the previous document from 2005), but the standards are listed again, this time by program, and, where relevant, practices are indicated in boxed sections.

Using the new document, there are some standards to which a school librarian could relate to, respond to, and take the initiative for implementing in a diploma context. They may not necessarily be the ones individual school librarians would choose, so it is advisable for librarians to look on the IB website for the whole document, or obtain the latest version from the IBDP coordinator.

The key or most obvious (or only) reference to the library occurs under the resources section in Standard B2. Point number six refers to resources in general, but it does mention the library specifically, in the context that a school needs a library to provide a central support to the program implementation. But let's look at the standards in the order in which they appear.

Standard A is concerned with philosophy in general. A library contribution could be that a librarian may ensure that library policies are part of the school policies that are communicated to the IB, and that library policies relate to the IB Mission Statement and important IB philosophies, not least of which being international mindedness and academic honesty. An innovative librarian may well recast library services and collection policy to further the aims of the school in support of its IB program. For example, a librarian can promote databases and web 2.0 products or communication sites to DP students. Innovation doesn't have to be about large, sweeping changes; it can include micro-change. Indeed if a library is not evolving, it could be argued that it is not working. Therefore, a librarian may just need to audit change and improvement that has occurred, and identify whether they have, in part, come about in support of IB needs.

The standard also refers to international mindedness. Schools need to have adequate resources and information so that students can inquire about the cultures, perspectives, and languages of people of other cultures. The IB also encourages international networking by IB world schools. Supporting international mindedness should be a major focus of an IB library. Documentation about an initial project or audit of items in the library collection and selection guidelines may be helpful documentation, and the library commitment to providing material to support the development of international mindedness should be recorded in library collection development policies and plans, together with any photographs of displays and copies of booklists. There are opportunities for librarians to communicate and network with other librarians in other countries, whether on the OCC or other electronic means, and any such communication could be included in any gathering of evidence for this standard.

Standard B is concerned with the organization of the school. It requires that all areas of the school should be aware and supportive of the aims and direction of the IB.

The school library and its librarian can help further this aim overtly by providing a relevant collection of materials for teachers' professional development as it relates to the IBDP (which is perhaps a hidden or largely unrecognized aspect of professional development for teachers). Perhaps the librarian can also provide a collection for parents. It is possible to provide material about the IB and its aims for students, even if it is simply displaying IB posters in the library or providing a list of library aspects of the learner profile elements or providing copies of the IB mission statement. Issues of *IB World* can be of interest to students, as can some texts about the IB including Mathews and Hill (2005), Peterson (2003), and writings by George Walker, the Chief Executive Emeritus of the IB (e.g., 2004).

It is in Standard B2 that the reference to the school library appears. There is a practices box inset in point six, and indicates that there should be enough relevant resources in the library to support the DP. What the point does not mention, however, is a role for the librarian. Nevertheless, the present statement, although brief, is important because it does not just require a school to be aware of the role of the library simply as a general support service or facility. The statement specifies that the school should be aware of role of the library as related to the implementation of the DP. It is the focus on the curriculum and, by extension, learning experiences, that is the important part of the sentence. It is really about what the *library* can do and is already doing to enhance the *curriculum*, rather than what the *school* can do for the *library*. It is more about process and outcomes, rather than input measures.

This standard also refers to the need for a school academic honesty policy and specifically indicates that a school needs to provide sufficient resources to enable students to undertake their individual extended essays, both of which could be key areas of input from both library and librarian. As we have seen, supporting the extended essay is perceived by many to be a prime role of the library and librarian. The library could make quite an impact on a school's audit for this standard or in documentation or in a response that the school needs to compile. The library contribution should focus not only on static resource factors, but should identify the services provided by a librarian—the tutorial, advisory, and supportive or scaffolding role of the librarian as a teacher and role model for students' research skills and other aspects of information literacy—together with being a key player in supporting high levels of academic honesty.

There is also a reference to concurrency of learning that could be interpreted as everyone working together—cooperating, collaborating—to provide authentic learning experiences for students, and again can be related to very specific activities, ranging from, for instance, a 30-minute presentation to ITGS students or working with a geography teacher to update library resources for case studies to speaking to a meeting of extended essay supervisors about how to encourage students to get as much out of the research process as possible.

Standard C focuses on curriculum, not least collaboration and learning needs and styles, specifically referring to conceptual understanding and development of skills and learner profile attitudes. These are all aspects of information literacy that are at the heart of a school library. The librarian could relate how the library supports and extends the learner profile in practical ways as supporting the main thrust of this standard. This last standard focuses on the symbiotic relationship between teacher and student, involving a relevant and helping learning environment; use of resources; and development of skills. A librarian could interpret this vision of teacher-student relations as involving and including both library and librarian.

One practical way of using the standards in an ongoing way is to produce an annual report of library activities that is specifically focused on diploma needs. If your school offers the IBDP as an option, this may involve the librarian separating IBDP library initiatives/activities from other activities. Of course, it is helpful to keep the report brief and use bullet points rather than sentences. The key strategy is to use the standards' descriptors and other important IB language and phrases (e.g., *concurrency of learning*) as headings in the report, so it is quite clear what educational aspects are being supported and enriched by library activity and support.

These standards have brief descriptions and are a set of aims that the school needs to work towards. As such, it is about negotiating; providing evidence; focusing on process and outcomes; communicating and looking for connections, all skills, and competencies that librarians have become adept at in a climate of accountability and rapid change. Goodban (2004), addressing quality assurance aspects of implementing the IBDP, noted that a fully trained and well-qualified librarian, ideally a teacher-librarian, was required for schools with IBDP programs. But it was noted that it is crucial for the librarian to have a comprehensive understanding of the IBDP, because the role of the library and librarian could impinge on many areas of the IBDP.

One librarian's take on the role of the IB librarian is that she remembered participants at IB library workshops "express a need to know how to be 'a good IB librarian.'" Her response was that to be a good IB librarian is "only an extension of being a good school librarian." The secret is to "know the curriculum, know the teachers, and know the students"; with that knowledge, librarians can promote themselves as "welcoming, cheerful, helpful and knowledgeable professional resource" persons (Clark, 2006, p. 44).

Instead of following guidelines that may be concerned with input measures, by relating to the IB standards and having a thorough knowledge of the IBDP in that school, the library and librarian can be involved in the IBDP educational process and outcomes. In some cases, the librarian can show links between learning, the educational process, and the library, and therefore, play a role as an integral member of the school's IBDP community.

APPENDIX 1: THEORY OF KNOWLEDGE RESOURCES FOR A SCHOOL LIBRARY

This is not a definitive list; hopefully, there would be discussion, cooperation, or perhaps collaboration between the TOK teaching team and the librarian about what would be useful in a TOK library collection. These suggestions are identified in relation to some key terms identified in the TOK course outline. (Arranging this list in such a manner was suggested by a similar format in a TOK list from the library at Geelong Grammar School, Australia.)

EMOTION (WAY OF KNOWING)

Bazan, Tony. *The power of social intelligence*. HarperCollins, 2002.
Bradbury, Travis, & Greaves, Jean. *The emotional intelligence quick book*. Fireside, 2005.
Evans, Dylan. *Emotion (A very short introduction series)*. Oxford, 2003.
Goleman, Daniel. *Emotional intelligence and working with emotional intelligence*. Bloomsbury, 2004.
Goleman, Daniel. *Social intelligence*. Bantam Dell, 2006.

LANGUAGE (WAY OF KNOWING)

Chomsky, Noam. *Language and mind*. Cambridge, 2006.
Crystal, David. *Words, words, words*. Oxford, 2007.
Matthews, Peter. *Linguistics (A very short introduction)*. Oxford, 2003.
Pinker, Steven. *The language instinct: How the mind creates language*. HarperCollins, 1994.
Pinker, Steven. *The stuff of thought: Language as a window into human nature*. Penguin, 2008.

SENSE PERCEPTION (WAY OF KNOWING)

Morris, Desmond. *People watching, the guide to body language*, 2nd ed. Vintage, 2002.
Naik, Anita. *Body talk*. Ticktock, 2009.

REASON (WAY OF KNOWING)

Mlodinow, Leonard. *The drunkard's walk: how randomness rules our lives.* Penguin, 2009.
Priest, Graham. *Logic (A very short introduction).* Oxford, 2001.
Robinson, Dave. *Introducing empiricism.* Totem Books, 2004.
Weston, Anthony. *A rulebook for arguments.* Hackett, 2000.

KNOWLEDGE

Blackburn, Simon. *Think.* Oxford, 1999.
de Bono, E. *Six thinking hats.* Penguin, 1985.
Pinker, S. *How the mind works.* Penguin, 1997.
Woolf, Alex. *Artificial intelligence.* Hodder & Stoughton, 2002.

TRUTH AND BELIEF

Lynch, Michael P. *True to life: Why truth matters.* The MIT Press, 2005.
Žižek, Slavoj. *On belief.* Routledge, 2001.

ETHICS

Barad, Judith. *The ethics of* Star Trek. HarperCollins, 2000.
Blackburn, Simon. *Being good: a short introduction to ethics.* Oxford, 2001.
Singer, Peter. *Writings on an ethical life.* HarperCollins, 2000.
Thompson, Mel. *Ethical theory.* Hodder Murray, 2005.

CRITICAL THINKING

Czerner, T. *What makes you tick? The brain in plain English.* Wiley, 2001.
Fisher, Alice. *Critical thinking: An introduction.* Cambridge University Press, 2001.
Sim, Stuart. *Introducing critical theory.* Icon Books, 2001.

EPISTEMOLOGY/THEORY OF KNOWLEDGE

Cardinal, Daniel. *Epistemology: The theory of knowledge.* John Murray, 2004.
Morton, Adam. *A guide through the theory of knowledge.* Blackwell, 1997.
Moser, Paul K., Mulder, Dwayne H., & Trout, J.D. *The theory of knowledge: A thematic introduction.* Oxford University Press, 1998.

PHILOSOPHICAL AND PSYCHOLOGICAL IDEAS

Abel, Reuben. *Man is the measure.* The Free Press, 1976.
Blackmore, Susan. *Consciousness (A very short introduction).* Oxford, 2003.
Cathcart, Thomas. *Plato and the platypus.* Penguin, 2007.
Craig, Edward. *Philosophy (A very short introduction).* Oxford, 2002.
Dupre, Ben. *50 philosophical ideas you really need to know.* Quercus, 2007.
Hamilton, Sue. *Indian philosophy (A very short introduction).* Oxford, 2001.
Horner, Chris. *Thinking through philosophy: An introduction.* Cambridge, 2000.

Janicaud, Dominique. *Philosophy in 30 days* (trans. from French). Granta Publications, 2005.

Kohn, Marek. *Trust: Self-interest and the common good.* Oxford, 2008.

Law, Stephen. *The philosophy files.* Orion, 2000.

Nisbett, Richard. *The geography of thought.* Free Press, 2004.

Pink, Thomas. *Free will (A very short introduction).* Oxford, 2004.

Pinker, Steven. *How the mind works.* W.W. Norton, 1997.

Pirsing, Robert M. *Zen and the art of motorcycle maintenance.* Vintage, 1991.

Robinson, Dave, & Judy Groves. *Introducing philosophy: A graphic guide to the history of thinking.* Totem Books, 2007.

Segal, Robert. *Myth (A very short introduction).* Oxford, 2004.

Slater, Lauren. *Opening Skinner's box: Great psychological experiments of the twentieth century.* Bloomsbury, 2004.

Smart, Ninian. *World philosophies.* Routledge, 1999.

AREAS OF KNOWLEDGE

Arnold, John. *History (A very short introduction).* Oxford, 2000.

Baker, Joanne. *50 physics ideas you really need to know.* Quercus, 2007.

Bassett, Bruce, & Ralph Edney. *Introducing relativity: A graphic guide.* Totem Books, 2009.

Best, Joel. *Damned lies and statistics: Untangling numbers from the media, politicians and activists.* University of California Press, 2001.

Black, Maggie. *No nonsense guide to international development.* New Internationalist, 2007.

Botton, Alain de. *A week at the airport.* Penguin, 2010.

Brooks, Michael. *13 things that don't make sense: The most baffling scientific mysteries of our time.* Doubleday, 2008.

Carr, E.H. *What is history?* Penguin, 1961.

Crilly, Joy. *50 mathematical ideas you really need to know.* Quercus, 2007.

Culler, Jonathan. *Literary theory (A very short introduction).* Oxford 1997.

Dixon, Thomas. *Science and religion (A very short introduction).* Oxford 2008.

Dolby, R.G.A. *Uncertain knowledge: An image of science for a changing world.* Cambridge, 1996.

Fukuyama, Francis. *The end of history and the last man.* Hamish Hamilton, 1999.

Goldacre, Ben. *Bad science.* Fourth Estate, 2008.

Hawkings, Stephen. *The universe in a nutshell.* Bantam Books, 2001.

Hoggan, James. *Climate cover-up: The crusade to deny global warming.* Greystone Books, 2009.

Klein, Naomi. *No logo.* HarperCollins, 2000.

Lesmoir-Gardo, Nigel, Will Rood, & Ralph Edney. *Fractals: A graphic guide.* Totem Books, 2009.

Macmillan, M. *The uses and abuses of history.* Profile Books, 2009.

Margulies, N. *Mapping inner space.* Zephyr Press, 2002.

Newton, Roger. *Thinking about physics.* Princeton University Press, 2000.

Okasha, Samuel. *Philosophy of science (A very short introduction).* Oxford, 2002.

Pennac, Daniel. *Rights of the reader.* Candlewick Press, 2008.

Rafferty, M. *100 books that shaped world history.* Bluewood Books, 2002.

Ravetz, Jerome. *The no-nonsense guide to science.* Verso, 2006.

Sardar, Ziauddin, & Borin Van Loon. *Introducing cultural studies.* Totem Books, 1998.

Sautoy, Marcus du. *The music of the primes: Why can unsolved problems in mathematics matter.* Harper, 2003.

Singh, Patwant. *The world according to Washington: An Asian view*. UGI Perspectives, 2004.

Singh, Simon. *Fermat's last theorem*. HarperCollins, 1998.

Smith, Leonard. *Chaos (A very short introduction)*. Oxford, 2007.

Stannard, Russell. *Relativity (A very short introduction)*. Oxford, 2008.

Swift, Richard. *The no-nonsense guide to democracy*. Verso, 2002.

Trigg, Roger. *Rationality and science: Can science explain everything?* Blackwell, 1993.

Wolke, Robert L. *What Einstein told his barber: More scientific answers*. Dell Publications, 2000.

GENERAL

Gaardner, Jostein. *Sophie's world: A novel about the history of philosophy*. Farrar, Straus & Giroux, 1991.

Lagemaat, Richard van de. *Theory of knowledge*. Cambridge, 2005.

McArthur's Universal Corrective Map of the World (upside-down map), Universal Press Pty. (Australia). Other maps include the Hobo-Dyer map (equal area projection), also available from http://www.odt.org; Peters Projection World maps, together with *A new view of the world: Handbook to the Peters Projection World maps*, 4th ed., due fall 2010 (available from http://www.petersmap.com).

Paul, Anthea. *Real girls' stories*. Allen & Unwin, 2004.

Zouev, Alexander. *Three: The ultimate student's guide to acing your Extended Essay and Theory of Knowledge*. Zouev Publishing, 2008.

DVDs

A Beautiful Mind, Universal Studios, 2001.

Bowling for Columbine, MGM, 2002.

Fahrenheit 9/11, Sony Pictures, 2004.

Fahrenhype 9/11, Trinity Home Entertainment, 2005.

An Inconvenient Truth, Paramount, 2006.

Lost in Translation, Universal Studios, 2004.

The Matrix, Warner, 1999.

Memento, Lions Gate, 2000.

Nell, 20th Century Fox, 1994.

Rabbit-proof Fence, Miramax, 2002.

Supersize me, Sony, 2004.

The Terminal, Dreamworks, 2004.

The Truman Show, Paramount, 1998.

Twelve Angry Men, MGM, 1957.

Vanilla Sky, Paramount, 2001.

What the Bleep Do We Know!?, 20th Century Fox, 2004.

PERIODICALS

In practice a wide range of periodicals may contain articles that would be useful for TOK purposes, but listed below are amongst those that are often mentioned:

Atlantic Monthly
The Economist
New Internationalist
New Scientist
Philosophy Now
Psychology Today
The Smithsonian
The World Today

APPENDIX 2: EXAMPLES OF LIBRARY INFORMATION FOR HELP-SHEETS AND LIBRARY WEBSITES

The librarian could produce help-sheets for students that relate specifically to certain resources, such as websites. Because periodicals may be a format not very familiar to students, here is an example of a help-sheet, addressed to students, that discusses how to evaluate periodical sources.

TIPS TO EVALUATE PERIODICAL SOURCES

You may find it helpful to include periodical articles in your extended essay. Periodicals are important because they can provide more current information than in book format. Periodicals references include essay-length articles on very specific aspects of a topic. You can get articles online as well as in print format, which is sometimes called "hard copy." Some periodicals are hosted on a publisher's website and may well charge for access to full-text articles, though you can usually read an abstract of the article for free on publishers websites. You can also read whole-text articles through databases that the school library subscribes to. You can find out what databases your school library subscribes to by checking the school library website. Alternatively, please ask the library staff to help you. They will be pleased to show you how the databases work.

Whether in hard copy or online, some of the following tips may help you to judge whether a periodical source is likely to provide you with useful information for your extended essay:

- Magazines that contain more serious information can more usually be referred to as journals, serials, or periodicals (you will probably find these terms used in university libraries).

- A serious periodical may have the world "journal" in its title (e.g., *Journal of Research in Applied Chemistry*).

- Periodicals are more likely to have a volume and/or an issue number (e.g., vol. 23, no. 1), and be published regularly, such as each month or every quarter of a year. (Sometimes the date will be printed in the periodical, but not always, so the volume and issue number can be very important.)

- The periodical will probably have an editorial board (the names of members may be printed inside the cover of the issue). The board is made up of experts in the field, whose job is to assess the articles received for publication.

- The best journal articles are those that report original research. Look for articles that are "peer-reviewed," or in other words, articles that have been reviewed by experts in a particular area (usually the board). The experts must agree that an article is worthy of publication before the article is accepted for publication. Sometimes, the review process results in recommendations that authors revise parts of the article before it can be accepted. If you hear or read the phrase "peer-reviewed journals," you know you can trust the articles in the journal concerned as being of very high quality.

- There should be a named author or authors for each article.

- There should be an abstract, which appears at the very beginning of the article. This provides brief information about the content and recommendations of the article. Reading this helps you judge whether the article is going to be useful to you.

- After the abstract, the article begins. A peer-reviewed article will usually contain the following elements: an introduction, indication of the research method used by the researcher(s), a description or account of the research, a discussion, and finally a conclusion.

- There should be a bibliography at the end of the article, together with citations in the text, and there may be an appendix or appendices. Appendices sometimes include documents that are relevant to the article, but cannot be included in the article, for various reasons.

Please ask the library for any help in assessing and obtaining periodical articles for your extended essay.

This is a very simple help-sheet that could be displayed in the library and perhaps also be on a screensaver.

HOW TO CITE OR REFERENCE A WEBSITE YOU HAVE USED IN ASSIGNMENTS

The basic order in the Harvard system is:

- Author (if this is available)
- Title (or heading on the web page)
- Date *you* consulted the website
- URL

Examples are:

Emory University. *Philip Glass* (20th century music composers). 30 May 2010. URL http://www.emory.edu/MUSIC/ARNOLD/glass.html

MLA Style on the Web. 5 July 2010. URL http://www.mla.org

Please look at the online guide to making a bibliography, which is available on the school library website, or ask the library staff for further help about citation and making a bibliography.

HOW TO USE THE SCHOOL LIBRARY TO ASSIST WITH GROUP 1 IBDP: A SHORT GUIDE FOR STUDENTS

This short information guide to using the literature section in the school library is to help IBDP Group 1 students to use the library more effectively and easily.

How to Find Specific Literature Texts and Information about Literature

Aspects of literature are classified in the nonfiction part of the school library according to the Dewey Decimal Classification (which is generally used in many libraries in the world). For literature, the base call number 800 is used. The following table will help you to find information in this section:

800   General information on literature and the theory of literature

808.5   Debating

808.82   Monologues

How to Find English Language Poetry, Drama, and Novelists

810   Literature in English (whether North American, Australian, British, Caribbean, etc.).

810.9   History of literature.

811   Poetry by individual poets. For example, if you want poems by Langston Hughes, look for the call number 811 HUG; if John Donne, look for 811 DON. As well as the poetry texts, books of biography and criticism about individual poets are kept at the same place, so you only have one section in which to look.

811.08   Books of anthologies of poetry—where poems are by more than one poet, and chosen or selected by an editor, perhaps on a theme or historical period, and so forth.

811.09   Anthologies of poetry about war.

812   Plays by individual dramatists. For example, if you want a play by of information about Wendy Wasserstein, look for 812 WAS; or Caryl Churchill, look for 812 CHU.

812.08   Anthologies of plays or drama-scripts, where the collection includes plays by more than one dramatist.

813   Critical works and biographies of novelists, for example, if you want to find information about the author Jane Austen, go to 813 AUS; if you want Nadine Gordimer, go to 813 GOR.

How to Find Novels or Short Fiction in the Library

Because there are so many novels and short fiction books, they are shelved in a separate section. The order is alphabetical by the author's last or family name (which is sometimes called a surname). In many schools, the fiction section is divided into two parts—one for younger students and the other for older students and adults in the school—and each section should be clearly labeled.

How to Find Information about Shakespeare

Because there are so many books about Shakespeare, they are also organized into a separate area, so that you may find information more easily: 822.3 is the main call number for works by and about Shakespeare. Then:

822.3 a–z. Individual plays. If you want the text or critical commentary or DVD of a play, they are grouped together, wherever possible. For example, for items regarding Hamlet, go to 822.3 HAM; for Romeo and Juliet, look for 822.3 ROM. Collected works are at 822.3 WOR.

822.303 General information about the plays.

822.307 Performing Shakespeare plays.

822.308 Retellings of plays.

822.309 Biographical and historical information about Shakespeare, the person.

How to Find Information about Non-English Literatures

These are the call numbers for other world literatures

830	German literature
839	Scandinavian literature
840	French literature
850	Italian literature
860	Spanish literature
870	Latin literature
880	Greek literature
891.7	Russian literature
895.1	Chinese literature
895.6	Japanese literature

WHAT OTHER RESOURCES ARE THERE IN THE LIBRARY TO ASSIST GROUP 1 STUDENTS?

- Reference material, such as encyclopedias and specialist reference items about literature, are all interfiled in the one nonfiction sequence.
- Don't forget to check out the periodical or magazine section, which may contain information relevant to your project, such as reviews and articles about works of literature and their writers.

- The language section (call number 400) has information about the history and development of language.
- The drama section (call number 792) has information about performing and producing works of literature on the stage and in film.
- It is worth checking online databases for digitized information. Check with the librarian to see which databases your library subscribes to.

Please ask the library staff for any further information.

APPENDIX 3: EXAMPLE OF LIBRARY BOOKLIST TO SUPPORT GROUP 1

"A SENSE OF PLACE": A LIST OF RECOMMENDED VACATION READING FOR NEW IBDP CANDIDATES

Atwood, Margaret. *Surfacing*. FIC ATW
   Detective story and thriller, set in a remote part of Canada.
Aw, Tash. *The Harmony Silk Factory*. FIC AW
   A family story set in Malaysia in 1940, presented from an indigenous point of view.
Bache-Wiig, Harald, Kjaerstad, Jan, & Bjerck, Birgit (Eds.). *Leopard VI: The Norwegian feeling for real*. FIC SHORT STORIES
   A collection of contemporary short stories from Norway.
Baricco, Alessandro. *Silk*. FIC BAR
   A French view of Meiji-period Japan.
Birch, Carol. *Come back, Paddy Riley*. FIC BIR
   A contemporary story of adolescent love and relationships.
Bowen, Elizabeth. *Eva Trout*. FIC POW
   An elegant comedy of manners that involves a realist heroine.
Drewe, Robert. *The bodysurfers*. FIC DRE
   Australian short stories all set on or around the beach.
Everett, Percival. *American desert*. FIC EVE
   A satire on contemporary culture.
Fitzgerald, Penelope. *The beginning of spring*. FIC FIT
   This story features an expatriate settled in Moscow who is uneasy about pre-revolutionary Russia.
Freud, Esther. *Summer at Gaglow*. FIC FRE
   A search for family truth, coupled with a sense of place and history—Eastern Germany.
Geras, Adele. *Other echoes*. FIC GER
   An evocation of a childhood in Borneo and the power of memories.
Hazard, Shirley. *The great fire*. FIC HAZ
   Set in occupied Japan, in the aftermath of the World War II, this story is concerned with love and a sense of humanity.
Ihimaera, Witi. *The uncle's story*. FIC IHI
   From a Maori point of view, Michael uncovers secrets about his uncle, who fought in the Vietnam War.

Ishiguro, Kazuo. *Never let me go.* FIC ISH
> Cloning, memory, and personal freedom are the themes of this evocative novel.

Judd, Alan. *The Kaiser's last kiss.* FIC JUD
> Set in the Netherlands during World War II, this novel presents a re-evaluation of values of a key character from World War I.

Koch, Christopher. *Highways to a war.* FIC KOC
> After a war photographer disappears in the Cambodian conflict, the story presents the person involved together with a sense of history of Cambodia.

Lahiri, Jhumpa. *The namesake.* FIC LAH
> Features an immigrant experience, highlighting cultural and generational issues.

Lapcharoensap, Rattawut. *Sightseeing.* FIC LAP
> A collection of stories from Thailand that explores issues of urbanization, globalization, traditional cultures, and youth versus age.

Mansfield, Katherine. *The garden party and other stories.* FIC MAN
> Short stories by a major author from New Zealand.

Martel, Yann. *Life of Pi.* FIC MAR
> An imaginative account of a shipwreck with animals, including a Bengal tiger and a 16-year-old Indian boy.

McCall Smith, Alexander. *The Sunday philosophy club.* FIC McC
> A mystery story set in Edinburgh, Scotland, with an integral discussion of ethics. The sense of place in this novel is a major element in the story.

Pérez-Reverte, Arturo. *The Flanders panel.* FIC PER
> A murder story and a thriller set in the art world of Madrid. Good sense of atmosphere and characterization.

Roa, G.V. *Krishna puppets.* FIC ROA
> Set in Andhra Pradesh, India, the novel portrays the effects of sudden change on the community.

Self, Will. *The quantity theory of insanity.* FIC SEL
> A novella and some short stories all linked by black satire.

Smith, Zadie. *The autograph man.* FIC SMI
> A comedy set in North London, United Kingdom, in the 1970s.

Thompson, Holly. *Ash.* FIC THO
> An evocation of place (southern Japan) from a crosscultural point of view.

Vargos Llosa, Mario. *Who killed Palomino Molero?* FIC VAR
> Set in Peru in the 1950s, this murder story shows how guilt, equality, and justice may or may not exist in a community.

Weiss, M. Jerry (ed). *Big city cool: Short stories about urban youth.* FIC SHORT STORIES
> Short stories about the urban experience in different parts of the United States.

West, Rebecca. *Cousin Rosamund.* FIC WES
> Reflection on the exuberance of youth, shown through contrasting periods—the exuberant 1920s, and the sober 1930s.

Zadok, Rachel. *Gem squash tokoloshe.* FIC ZAD
> A first-person account of apartheid in Northern Transvaal, South Africa.

APPENDIX 4: INFORMATION LITERACY–RELATED RESEARCH CONCERNING THE IBDP

These studies relate to students and how they learn and are supported in their IBDP candidacy. Please note that full details are provided in the bibliography. Most are studies from the general education scene; some are practitioner based. The few studies that emanate from the LIS sector are indicated by an asterisk next to the author's names. Most of these selected pieces of research are cited several times in the text and are included here with summaries of for reference and greater convenience of readers.

Burris, Welner, Wiley, & Murphy, 2007
Article title: *A world-class curriculum for all: Does encouraging more students to take International Baccalaureate classes force teachers to lower their standards? Not when students have the right preparation and support.*

This study focused on use of the IBDP to provide entry into better tertiary institutions in the United States for a broad ability range of students. Findings, based on one school district in New York, particularly identified benefits to students of ethnicities who were underrepresented in existing "rigorous courses" (p. 53). Important strategies were preparing and motivating students in years prior to the IBDP and ensuring ethnically mixed classes. Also, supporting students through increased "resource duty" by teachers, who also prepared materials as scaffolding techniques—such as "instead of requiring students to read numerous supplementary texts in their entirety for IB History, teachers identified and assigned the most crucial excerpts from the texts" (p. 55). Subject classes and the full diploma were distinguished, though no mention was made of core aspects. As support and resources were identified, a role for a library and librarian might have been expected, but none was mentioned, nor of skills gained from the program.

Kyburg, Hertberg-Davis, & Callaghan, 2007
Article title: *Advanced Placement and International Baccalaureate programs: Optimal learning environments for talented minorities?*

A grounded theory study of interviews with teachers and focus groups of students concerning AP and IB courses. Whilst teaching and learning styles varied, fast-paced lecture-style teaching delivered significant content and allowed student questioning, but there was pressure to "teach to the exams" (p. 12). Students were "challenge-seeking, motivated, well-prepared, multi-taskers, confident, compliant, high achievers, good time managers" (p. 19) who perceived peer support as an added benefit, and who looked to the IBDP to help them enter better or preferred institutions of tertiary education. The researchers considered that the IBDP was not appropriate for "students without mastery of requisite skills (good study habits, motivation, writing skills)" (p. 26) who needed to develop "skills/attitudes necessary for success" (p. 29) prior to commencing the diploma. Theories were developed about peer support, supportive faculty who employed a flexible range of teaching strategies, students' abilities to manage their work, and "supportive adults." (Whilst it is possible to infer a role for the library and librarian, none was identified.) IB programs, rather than the diploma per se, were referred to in the report, suggesting that both certificate and diploma options were common.

Latuputty, 2005 *

Paper title: *Improving the school library for IB students: A case study at the British International School, Jakarta.*

This practitioner study was based on an international school in Indonesia, where most of the older students undertook the diploma. She found that students used the library because they needed quiet study accommodation. Resources most used were reference and audiovisual items, often related to history topics (and were used either in class or at home). Many diploma students were unaware of or had not used subscription databases and used computers in the library mainly for accessing the Internet. Most students "found the librarians were helpful, nice, readily answered their questions and close to students" (p. 18). She surveyed students after they had completed their extended essay, to ensure that the students surveyed had already undertaken research and used the school library. Most students had used nonfiction references. Some could not find items they needed. However, students perceived that their research skills were adequate. Librarians accessed resources and facilitated contact with external sources of information for students, such as a local university library.

McGregor & Streitenberger, 1998 *

Article title: *Do scribes learn?: Copying and information use.*

This North American study of plagiarism was in the context of a gifted program, though the diploma was identified. The study led the researchers to question whether student learning could improve "if librarians and teachers work more closely together to mediate in the library research experience." In particular, would more or "different collaboration between teachers and librarians have an impact on information use?" (p. 18). Little adult intervention (including the librarian) in students' research activities was observed, and there was an assumption that "students knew how to use information without assistance" and had prior experience of doing so, including paraphrasing and citing skills (p. 9).

Munro, 2003

Article: *The influence of student learning characteristics on progress through the extended essay, a component of the International Baccalaureate Diploma Programme.*

Munro identified a link between TOK and the extended essay in a study of Australian IBDP students, in terms of understanding and making their own knowledge. Munro went much further in identifying skills developed in and required by the essay: to be successful in offering new hypotheses, students needed motivation and self-management for independent learning; time management; creative thinking; framing, discussing, and answering their own questions; developing information literacy by being aware of previous knowledge; selecting, organizing, and evaluating knowledge (pp. 6–7).

Paris, 2003

Article: *The International Baccalaureate: A case study on why students choose to do the IB.*

Some grade 10 students perceived that IBDP would be stressful when considering following it or another option (their state certificate in South Australia) and that high-level organizational skills are required for success in the IBDP. Student opinions were grouped by their perceptions of both programs but there was little difference except they considered the diploma to be better for development of values and attitudes. Categories developed for this research were broad, and did not specifically identify features such as critical thinking and time management.

Rafste, 2003 *

Article: *A place to learn or a place for leisure: Pupils' use of the school library in Norway.*

This Norwegian study focused on socialization, but one of the two libraries included in the study was in a school that offered the IBDP. Rafste studied library use by students at two schools. The one specific mention of the diploma concerned occupancy of the library by IBDP students. Overall, first-year IBDP students used the library least, while second-year IBDP students used it most.

Shaunessy, Suido, Hardesty, & Shatter, 2006

Article: *School functioning and psychological well-being of International Baccalaureate and general education students: A preliminary examination.*

The researchers studied psychological aspects of IBDP candidates and other students in the same schools in North America and found that non-IBDP students considered themselves slightly disadvantaged in terms of school resources (though library provision was not specifically mentioned). However, the diploma students did not feel more pressure than non-IBDP students, though the former tended to a more cohesive, highly motivated social group.

Snapper, 2006

Paper: *Marked for life? Progression from the IBDP.*

In a retrospective qualitative study, Snapper found that nine former students in the United Kingdom developed a range of skills and qualities, including maturity, self-confidence, time management, and the ability to work independently and collaboratively. These students found the first year of university life less stressful because of the skills, work-load experience, and expectations developed as diploma candidates.

Taylor, Pogrebin, & Dodge, 2002

Article: *Advanced Placement—advanced pressures: Academic dishonesty among elite high school students.*

This study examined academic dishonesty amongst students of AP and IB courses in the United States. The focus of the study was on schools where such courses were optional. Students prioritized academic success; pressure came from teachers, perceived competition from other students, and limited time. Most positively, IB students supported each other informally; negatively, they colluded or exchanged answers for assignments. Students understood plagiarism variously. For example, copying from others or a printed source was not considered a serious issue and it was accepted that such practices necessarily occurred. Thus, it was found that "dishonest academic methods were frequently utilized by the elite high school students" (p. 407).

Taylor & Porath, 2006

Article: *Reflections on the International Baccalaureate Program: Graduates' perspectives.*

Taylor and Porath studied 16 Canadian IBDP graduates in relation to gifted education. Although not designed specifically for gifted students, the diploma was one of few available programs. About a quarter of IBDP graduates considered that the workload was "excessive, unmanageable, and/or detrimental to their well-being" (p. 153), though made positive comments about developing time management skills, critical thinking skills, organizational and communication skills, and "a strong work ethic" (p. 154). Students felt that the experiences they gained were helpful for higher education, and students noted support from peers, teachers, and family. No mention of a library or librarian was made.

Tekle, 2005

Thesis title: *The International Baccalaureate Diploma Programme (IBDP) at Katedralskolan, Uppsala: A study with emphasis on how the programme functions and on the teaching of geography.*

Tekle found "a general feeling of stress" at the Katedralskolan, Uppsala, Swedish school during students' first year of the diploma that led some students to consider changing to less-pressured courses. However, most students continued with the IBDP, which they found demanding (especially for students whose English language skills were developing) and required good levels of time management, not least for reading. Students indicated that they felt they had "grown as adults" during the program (p. 16). Tekle specifically studied the effect of the geography course, where teachers did not have the experience of selecting material in English from other countries. Students could borrow books and some students found difficulty in reading, interpreting text, and extracting relevant information, and needed assistance from teachers. No mention of a librarian or library was made.

Tilke, 2009 *

Thesis title: *Factors affecting the impact of a library and information service on the International Baccalaureate Diploma Programme in an international school: A constructivist grounded theory approach.*

A practitioner study of students experiences through the two years of their candidature for the IBDP, focused on an international school in Asia, where all grade 11–12 students were IBDP candidates. There were 22 participants in the study, who included students (who were users and non-users of the school library), teachers, and administrators. The detail of the study and findings inform the main text of this book.

Vanderbrook, 2006

Article: *Intellectually gifted females and their perspectives of lived experience in the AP and IB programs.*

Vanderbrook studied one diploma and one certificate student in North America and found they spent most time with fellow IB students, rather than with other students in the same school. Time management was an issue; mastery of significant subject content, workload, and grades were main concerns. Teachers were cited as significant influences as were "intellectual peers" (p. 143), both for academic and emotional support. There was one reference to the school library, where the diploma student often studied for classes with friends in the library. There was no mention of the extended essay in this study, though there was no indication at what stage the IBDP program was when the study occurred.

APPENDIX 5: BOOKS ON ESSAY WRITING, THE EXTENDED ESSAY, AND ABSTRACTS

Beall, Herbert. (2001). *A short guide to writing about chemistry*. New York: Longman.

Cuba, Lee. (2002). *A short guide to writing about social science*. New York: Longman.

Hacker, Diana. (2008). *Rules for writers*. 6th ed. Boston, MA: Bedford/St. Martin's Press.

Hacker, Diana. (2007). *A writer's reference*. 6th ed. Boston, MA: Bedford/St. Martin's Press.

Lipson, Charles. (2006). *Cite right: A quick guide to citations styles: MLA, APA, Chicago, etc.* Chicago University Press.

Marius, Richard. (2002). *A short guide to writing about history*. 4th ed. New York: Longman.

Shiach, Don. (2009). *How to write essays: A step-by-step guide for all levels, with sample essays*. 2nd ed. Oxford: How To Books.

Szuchman, Lenore T. (2010). *Writing with style: APA style made easy*. 5th ed. Belmont, CA: Wadsworth.

Timmer, Joseph. (1996). *The essentials of MLA style*. Boston, MA: Houghton Mifflin.

Zouev, Alexander. (2008). *Three: The ultimate student's guide to acing your Extended Essay and Theory of Knowledge*. n.p.: Zouev Publishing.

BOOKS TO HELP WITH WRITING THE ABSTRACT

Alfred, Gerald J., Brusaw, Charles T., & Oliu, Walter E. (2006). *Handbook of technical writing*. New York: St. Martin's Press.

Dunkley, S., Banham, D., & Macfarlane, A. (2006). Mathematics and the sciences. In Tim Pound (Ed.), *The International Baccalaureate Diploma Programme: An introduction for teachers and managers* (pp. 115–146.). London: Routledge. (For a recommended example of an abstract.)

International Baccalaureate Organization. (2010). *Diploma Programme: Extended essay guide*. Cardiff: Author.

APPENDIX 6: EXAMPLE OF A POLICY ON DONATION OF IBDP EXTENDED ESSAYS TO THE SCHOOL LIBRARY

As with other items held in the school library collections, resources should be relevant to the needs of the school, its curriculum, and its ethos. Items donated to the library are accepted on this basis.

In line with relevant school library policies, it is accepted that resources may need to be withdrawn from the library (mainly because of currency/relevance, physical deterioration of the item, limited space in the library, etc.).

Traditionally, a copy of each student's extended essay is held in the school library. Extended essays from previous years are promoted to the current grade 11 students as models and examples of good practice. Each extended essay that received a grade A, B, or C has been thus annotated in the library collection.

All extended essays are kept for two years after the individual student has graduated from the school. Those kept after that time are held because the essay is:

- graded A, B, or C,
- in a subject area that is less well-represented by extended essays, or
- about the school.

Items fitting such criteria will be catalogued on the automated library management system.

APPENDIX 7: GLOSSARY OF IB ACRONYMS AND TERMINOLOGY

ab initio   Course in Group 2 for students who have no previous experience of a language.

academic honesty   Important IB document relating to the IBDP.

AoK   Area(s) of Knowledge, a key term in the TOK course.

A1   Language A1, group 1 of the IBDP subject matrix.

authorization   Process that schools undertake in order to offer an IB program.

candidate   Student enrolled in the IBDP.

Cardiff   Location of the IB Curriculum and Assessment Center.

CAS   Creativity, action, and service.

certificate   An IB Certificate may be awarded to a student who completes requirements and sits final examinations in specific subjects only. For a certificate, students do not complete full diploma requirements (i.e., they do not undertake TOK, extended essay, and CAS).

concurrency of learning   Involves collaboration with and amongst teachers; team teaching.

continuum   A key aspect of IB philosophy, referring to the continuum of education through the three IB programs, covering student ages 5–18 years.

continuum school   School that offers three IB programs.

coordinator   The IB requires schools to appoint a member of faculty to coordinate each IB program that it offers.

core   Comprises CAS, extended essay, and TOK. All diploma candidates need to complete these requirements to pass IBDP.

DP   Diploma program.

experimental sciences   Group 4 of the IBDP subject matrix.

EE   Extended essay.

45   Maximum points for a diploma.

HL   Higher level (subject option).

IB(O)   International Baccalaureate (Organization).

IBA   International Baccalaureate Americas (region of the IB).

IBAP   International Baccalaureate Asia Pacific (region of the IB).

IBAPLIS   International Baccalaureate Asia Pacific Library and Information Specialists (group).

IBCA   International Baccalaureate Curriculum & Assessment Center of the IB.

IBDP   International Baccalaureate Diploma Programme.

IBEAM   International Baccalaureate Europe, Africa, and the Middle East (region of IB).

IBVC   International Baccalaureate Virtual Community.

IB World   House magazine of the IB.

individuals & societies   Group 3 of the IBDP subject matrix.

internal assessment   A coursework requirement for subject options.

ITGS   Information technology in a global society (Group 3 subject option).

JRIE   *Journal of Research in International Education*, a research periodical that has strong support from the IB.

knower(s)   Key term at the heart of the TOK course.

language B   Group 2 of the IBDP subject matrix.

LP   Learner profile.

MYP   Middle Years Programme.

OCC   Online Curriculum Center.

programme standards   Schools need to meet or work towards these benchmarks (full name: IB Programme Standards and Practices) in order to offer IB programs.

PYP   Primary Years Programme.

SL   Standard level (subject option).

subject matrix   Comprises six subject groups that students must study.

supervisor   Each student needs a supervisor for her/his extended essay.

TCK   Third-culture kids. Not specifically an IB term, but TCK may well be students who follow IB programs.

3   Refers to the points awarded for core requirements of the diploma.

TOK   Theory of Knowledge.

24   Candidates need to achieve 24 points in order to be awarded a diploma.

Vade Mecum   Former name of IBDP regulation manual. Term no longer used by IB.

viva   Interview that a student can have with her/his supervisor at the end of his/her extended essay process.

WoK   Way(s) of Knowing, a key term in the TOK course.

workshops   A requirement for teachers and librarians who are involved in the IBDP.

world literature   A significant aspect of the A1 (group 1 of the IBDP subject matrix) course.

world school   School that has been authorized to offer an IB program.

REFERENCES

Please note that documents issued by the IB, such as academic honesty, learner profile, and standards, are not included in the bibliography. This is because it is essential that the latest versions of IB official documents are consulted. These are always available on the online curriculum center, through the IB website, and will also be available from a school's IBDP coordinator.

American Association of School Librarians. (2007). *Standards for the 21st century learner*. Chicago: American Library Association.

American Association of School Librarians. (2009). *Standards for the 21st century learner in action*. Chicago: American Library Association.

Andain, I., Rutherford, J., & Allen, P. (2006). Implementing the IBDP: Three retrospective accounts. In T. Pound (Ed.), *The International Baccalaureate diploma programme: An introduction for teachers and managers* (pp. 47–68). London: Routledge.

Anderson, T. (1994). The International Baccalaureate model of content-based art education. *Art Education, 47*(2), 19–24.

Asselin, M. (2005). Preparing preservice teachers as members of information literate school communities. In J. Henri & M. Asselin (Eds.), *Information literate school community, Vol. 2: Issues of leadership* (pp. 187–201). Wagga Wagga, Australia: Charles Sturt University.

Austin, S. (2006). The core components. In T. Pound (Ed.), *The International Baccalaureate diploma programme: An introduction for teachers and managers* (pp. 147–170). London: Routledge.

Australian School Library Association & Australian Library and Information Association. (2001). *Learning for the future: Developing information services in schools* (2nd ed.). Carlton, South Australia: Curriculum Corporation.

Barranoik, L. (2001). Research success with senior high school students. *School Libraries Worldwide, 7*(1), 28–45.

Barrett, L., & Douglas, J. (2004). *CILIP guidelines for secondary school libraries* (2nd ed.). London: Facet Publishing.

Bartlett, S., Burton, D., & Peim, N. (2001). *Introduction to education studies*. London: Paul Chapman Publishing.

Bland, J.A., & Woodworth, K.R. (2009). *Case studies of participation and performance in the IB Diploma Programme.* Menlo Park,CA: Center for Education Policy, SRI International.

Boekhorst, A.K., & van Veen, M.J.P. (2001). School libraries in the Netherlands. *School Libraries Worldwide, 7*(1), 82–102.

Branch, J.L., & Oberg, D. (2001). The teacher-librarian in the 21st century: The teacher-librarian as instructional leader. *School Libraries in Canada, 21*(2), 9–11.

Brown, A., & Laverty, C. (2001, November). *The changing role of IB librarians in the age of technology.* Paper presented at IBAP Librarians Workshop, Singapore, November 2000. Retrieved from http://educ.queensu.ca/~brownan/organizations/IB/Internet/IBAP/Sessions/ChangingRoleOfIBLibrarians/ChangingRole.htm

Buchanan, S., Douglas, L., Hachlaf, K., Varner, E., & Williams, P. (2005). *Evaluating the International Baccalaureate Programme: An IB proposal for the consideration of the North Vancouver School District.* (Unpublished master's thesis). University of British Columbia, Canada. Retrieved from http://slc.educ.ubc.ca/Masters/Buchannan.pdf

Burke, L. (2005). A case for international mindfulness. *International Schools Journal, 25*(1), 7–14.

Burris, C.C., Welner, K.G., Wiley E.W., & Murphy, J. (2007). A world-class curriculum for all: Does encouraging more students to take International Baccalaureate classes force teachers to lower their standards? Not when students have the right preparation and support. *Educational Leadership, 64*(7), 53–56.

Cairo American College. (2010). *CAC IB program.* Retrieved from http://www.cacegypt.org/hs/ib.html#diploma

Callison, D. (2005). Enough already? Blazing new trails for school library research: An interview with Keith Curry Lance, Director, Library Research Service, Colorado State Library & University of Denver. Interview questions and discussion by Daniel Callison, Professor, Indiana University, Indianapolis, and editor of School Library Media Research. *School Library Media Research.* Retrieved from the American Library Association website: http://www.ala.org/ala/aasl/aaslpubsandjournals/slmrb/editorschoiceb/lance/interviewlance.htm & http://www.ala.org/ala/aaslbucket/slmr/lance.htm

Cambridge, J., & Thompson, J. (2004). Internationalism and globalization as contexts for international education. *Compare, 34*(2), 161–175. Retrieved from the International Baccalaureate Organization website: www.ibo.org/programmes/research/members/documents/cambridgethompson-compare.pdf

Carber, S., & Reis, S. (2004). Commonalities in International Baccalaureate practice and the school-wide enrichment model. *Journal of Research in International Education, 3*(3), 339–359.

Charmaz, K. (2006). *Constructing grounded theory: A practical guide through qualitative analysis.* London: Sage Publications.

Chris, J. (1999). The effect of the IB on one comprehensive high school. *IB World, 16,* 33–35.

Clark, C. (1995). The school library: An under-used resource for the IB programme? *IB World, 9,* 43–46.

Clark, C. (2006). IB, the sixth form and the LRC: An international school perspective. In G. Dubber (Ed.), *Sixth sense: The sixth form and the LRC* (pp. 40–44). Swindon, UK: School Library Association.

Clarke, M. (2002). Response to Simon Murray's article: 2. *IB Research Notes, 2,* 11.

Coates, H., Rosicka, C., & MacMahon-Bell, M. (2007). *Perceptions of the International Baccalaureate Diploma Programme among Australian and New Zealand universities.* Canberra, Australia: Australian Council for Educational Research.

Coffey, M. (2006). Language, literature and the arts. In T. Pound (Ed.), *The International Baccalaureate diploma programme: An introduction for teachers and managers* (pp. 90–114). London: Routledge.

Coish, D. (2005). *Canadian school libraries and teacher-librarians: Results from the 2003/04 Information and Communications Technologies in Schools Survey.* Ottawa, Canada: Statistics Canada.

Combes, B., & Sekulla, G. (2002). Creating online curriculum: Effective partnerships. *School Libraries Worldwide, 8*(2), 38–50.

Committee of Librarians of IBO Schools. (1997, October 10–12). Report of a meeting held at the International Baccalaureate Curriculum & Assessment Center, Cardiff, Wales.

Cordoba, C.A. (1994). El rol de la biblioteca escolar en el Bachillerato Internacional [The role of the school library in the International Baccalaureate]. *IB World, 5,* 36–37.

Croft, S., & Cross, H. (2003). *English for the IB Diploma.* Oxford: Oxford University Press.

Dando, P. (2004, November 1). *IB Librarians' networking session.* Retrieved from www.ibmidatlantic.org/librarians_notes.pdf

Daniel, E. (1997, July). High school to university: What skills do students need? In L. Lightall & K. Haycock (Eds.), *Information rich but knowledge poor? Emerging issues for schools and libraries worldwide* (pp. 53–61). Seattle, WA: International Association of School Librarianship.

Day, K. (2010). A global reading list for hs. Retrieved from http://www.worldcat.org/profiles/KatherineDay/tags/global%20reading%20list%20for%20HS

Dickinson, A. (1997). The examiners speak. *IB World, 15,* 27.

Drake, B. (2004). International education and IB programmes: Worldwide expansion and potential cultural dissonance. *Journal of Research in International Education, 3*(2), 207–224.

Dunkley, S., Banham, D., & Macfarlane, A. (2006). Mathematics and the sciences. In T. Pound (Ed.), *The International Baccalaureate diploma programme: An introduction for teachers and managers* (pp. 115–146). London: Routledge.

Ellis, J., & Salisbury, F. (2004). Information literacy milestones: Building upon the prior knowledge of first-year students, *Australian Library Journal, 53*(4). Retrieved from the Australian Library & Information Association website: http://alia.org.au/publishing/alj/53.4/full.text/ellis/salisbury.html

Elwan, D.I. (1989). To what extent did the alliance of Ibn Sa'ud and the Ikhwan during the 1920s lead to the achievement of their respective goals? *The Concord Review: Special International Baccalaureate Issue, 1991,* 109–123. Retrieved from http://www.tcr.org/tcr/essays.htm

Everhart, N. (2000). An evaluation of the documents provided to school library media specialists by state library and educational agencies. *School Library Media Research, 3.* Retrieved from the American Library Association website: http://ala.org/ala/aasl/aaslpubsandjournals/slmrb/slmrcontents/volume32000/statedocs.htm

Everhart, N. (2006). Principals' evaluation of school librarians: A study of strategic and non-strategic evidence-based approaches. *School Libraries Worldwide, 12*(2), 38–51.

Farmer, L. (2005). Generating change: A North American perspective. In J. Henri & M. Asselin (Eds.), *Information literate school community, Vol. 2: Issues of leadership* (pp. 147–158). Wagga Wagga, Australia: Charles Sturt University.

Farmer, L. (2006). Library media program implementation and student achievement. *Journal of Librarianship & Information Science, 38*(1), 21–32.

Fitzgerald, M.A., & Galloway, C. (2003). Information literacy skills of college-level virtual library users: An exploratory study. In D. Callison (Ed.), *Measuring Student Achievement and Diversity in Learning: Papers of the Treasure Mountain Research Retreat #10 at the Elms, Excelsior Springs, Missouri, May 31–June 1, 2002* (pp. 181–205). Salt Lake City, UT: Hi Willow Research & Publishing.

Fox, E. (1998). The emergence of the International Baccalaureate as an impetus for curriculum reform. In M. Hayden & J. Thompson (Ed.), *International education: Principles and practice* (pp. 65–76). London: Kogan Page.

Frew, S. (2006). Private study or private play? Sixth formers' use of the school library. In G. Dubber (Ed.), *Sixth sense: The sixth form and the LRC* (pp. 45–56). Swindon, UK: School Library Association.

Goodban, J. (2004). Quality assurance and maintenance of the International Baccalaureate Diploma Programme. In M. van Loo & K. Morley (Eds.), *Implementing the IB Diploma Programme: A practical manual for principals, IB coordinators, heads of department and teachers* (pp. 9–30). Cambridge, UK: Cambridge University Press.

Goodin, M.E. (1991). The transferability of library research skills from high school to college. *School Library Media Quarterly, 20*(1), 33–42.

Hardman, S. (1994). Spoken Canadian English: Regional variations and national characteristics. *IB World, 6,* 18–23.

Hay, L. (2005). Student learning through Australian school libraries, part 1: A statistical analysis of student perceptions. *Synergy, 3*(2), 17–30. Retrieved from http://www.slav.schools.net.au/synergy/vol3num2/hay.pdf

Hay, L. (2006). Student learning through Australian school libraries, part 2: What students define and value as school library support. *Synergy, 4*(2), 27–38.

Hayden, M., & Thompson, J. (1995). International schools and international education: A relationship reviewed. *Oxford Review of Education, 21*(3), 327–345.

Hayden, M.C., Rancic, B.A., & Thompson, J.J. (2000). Being international: Student and teacher perceptions from international schools. *Oxford Review of Education, 26*(1), 107–123.

Hayden, M., & Wong, C. (1997). The International Baccalaureate: International education and cultural preservation. *Educational Studies, 23*(3), 349–362.

Head, A.J., & Eisenberg, M.B. (2009). Finding context: What today's college students say about conducting research in the digital age. *Project Information Literacy Progress Report, February 4, 2009.* Retrieved from www.projectinfolit.org/pdfs/PIL_ProgressReport_2_2009.pdf

Hepworth, M. & Walton, J. (2009). *Teaching information literacy for inquiry-based learning.* Oxford, UK, Chandos Publishing.

Henri, J., & Boyd, S. (2002). Teacher librarian influence: Principal and teacher librarian perspectives. *School Libraries Worldwide, 8*(2), 1–17.

Hill, I. (2003). The International Baccalaureate. In G. Phillips & T. Pound (Eds.), *The baccalaureate: A model for curricular reform* (pp. 47–75). London: Kogan Page.

Hunter, C., Payne, A., & Hobman, D. (2004). Group 4: Experimental sciences. In M. van Loo & K. Morley (Eds.), *Implementing the IB Diploma Programme: A practical manual for principals, IB coordinators, heads of department and teachers* (pp. 361–428). Cambridge, UK: Cambridge University Press.

International Baccalaureate Mid-Atlantic Sub-Regional Coalition. (2006). *Notes of librarians' meeting.* Retrieved from http://www.ibmidatlantic.org

International Baccalaureate Organization. (2002). *Diploma Programme,* Monograph. Geneva, Switzerland: IBO.

International Baccalaureate Organization. (2009). *IB and higher education: Developing policy for the IB Diploma program examinations, version 3, December 2009.* Retrieved from www.ibmidatlantic.org/IB_and_Higher_Education_Policy.pdf

International Baccalaureate Organization. (2010a). *IB World Statistics and IB Americas.* Retrieved from http://www.ibo.org/facts/fastfacts/

International Baccalaureate Organization. (2010b). *High school student engagement among IB and non-IB students in the United States: a comparison study.* Retrieved from http://www.ibo.org/research/programmevalidation/index.cfm#HSSSE

Irving, C. (2006). The identification of information literacy skills which students bring to university. *Library & Information Research, 30*(9), 47–54.

Jones, S. (2004a). Implementing the diploma programme in school. In M. van Loo & K. Morley (Eds.), *Implementing the IB Diploma Programme: A practical manual for principals, IB coordinators, heads of department and teachers* (pp. 31–77). Cambridge, UK: Cambridge University Press.

Jones, S. (2004b). The extended essay. In M. van Loo & K. Morley (Eds.), *Implementing the IB Diploma Programme: A practical manual for principals, IB coordinators, heads of department and teachers* (pp. 195–210). Cambridge, UK: Cambridge University Press.

Kenney, B. (2006). Ross to the rescue! Rutger's Ross Todd's quest to renew school libraries. *School Library Journal.* Retrieved from http://www.schoollibraryjournal.com/article/CA6320013.html

KRC Research. (2003). *A report of findings from six focus groups with K-12 parents, teachers, and principals, as well as middle and high school students.* Retrieved from the American Library Association website: www.ala.org/ala/aasl/proftools/@yourlib campaign/krc_research_report.pdf

Kuhlthau, C.C. (2004). *Seeking meaning: A process approach to library and information services* (2nd ed.). Westport, CN: Libraries Unlimited.

Kyburg, R.M., Hertberg-Davis, H., & Callahan, C.M. (2007). Advanced Placement and International Baccalaureate programs: Optimal learning environments for talented minorities? *Journal of Advanced Academics, 18*(2) 172–215.

Langford, L. (1998). Just what does a graduating secondary school student look like? *Access, 9,* 15–17.

Latrobe, K., & Havenar, W.M. (1997). The information-seeking behaviour of high school honors students: An exploratory study. *Journal of Youth Services in Libraries, 10*(2), 188–200.

Latuputty, H. (2005, July). Improving the school library for IB students: A case study at the British International School, Jakarta. In S. Lee, P. Warning, D. Singh, E. Howe, L. Farmer & S. Hughes (Eds.), *IASL Reports, 2005: Information Leadership in a Culture of Change, Selected Papers from the 34th Annual Conference of the Association of School Librarianship and the 9th International Forum on Research in School Librarianship, Incorporating IB PanAsia Library Media Specialists (IB PALMS), Hong Kong, China, July 8–12, 2005* [CD-ROM]. Hong Kong, China: International Association of School Librarianship.

Lear, A. (2002). The International Baccalaureate (IB): What is it? How might it affect school libraries in the UK. *School Libraries in View, 17,* 9–12.

Le Metais, J. (2002). *International developments in upper secondary education: Context, provision and issues.* Slough, UK: National Foundation for Educational Research.

Levin, D., & Arafeh, S. (2002). *The digital disconnect: The widening gap between Internet-savvy students and their schools, Pew Internet & American Life Project.* Retrieved from the Pew Internet Organization website: http://www.pewinternet.org/pdfs/PIP_Schools_Internet_Report.pdf

Limberg, L., & Alexandersson, M. (2003). The school library as a space for learning. *School Libraries Worldwide, 9*(1), 1–15.

Lonsdale, M. (2003). *Impact of school libraries on student achievement: A review of the research, report for the Australian School Libraries Association.* Retrieved from the Australian School Libraries Association website: http://www.asla.org.au/research/index.htm

Madden, A.D., Ford, N.J., & Miller, D. (2007). Information resources used by children at an English secondary school: perceived and actual levels of usefulness. *Journal of Documentation, 63*(3), 340–358.

Markuson, C. (1999). *Effective libraries in international schools: European Council of International Schools.* Saxmundham, UK: John Catt Educational.

Mathews, J., & Hill, I. (2005). *Supertest: How the International Baccalaureate can strengthen our schools.* Chicago: Open Court Publishing Company.

McCluskey, M. (2006). *Results of a survey on the provision of non-English language materials in international school libraries.* (Unpublished master's thesis). Robert Gordon University, Aberdeen, Scotland.

McGregor, J., & Streitenberger, D.C. (1998). Do scribes learn?: Copying and information use. *School Library Media Research 1998, 1.* Retrieved from the American Library Association website: http://www.ala.org/Content/NavigationMenu/AASL/Publications_and_Journals/School_Library_Media_Research/Contents1/Volume_1_(1998)_SLMQ_Online/mcgregor.htm

McKenzie, C.M. (2001). *The Victorian Certificate of Education, the Monash University Foundation Year Program and the International Baccalaureate: Choosing a course as preparation for tertiary study.* (Unpublished doctoral dissertation). Monash University, Clayton, Australia.

McLelland, D., & Crawford, J. (2004). The Drumchapel Project: A study of ICT usage by school pupils and teachers in a secondary school in a deprived area of Glasgow. *Journal of Librarianship & Information Science, 36*(2), 55–67.

Mellon, C.A. (1986). Library anxiety: A grounded theory and its development. *College & Research Libraries, 47,* 160–165.

Merchant, L., & Hepworth, M. (2002). Information literacy of teachers and pupils in secondary schools. *Journal of Librarianship & Information Science, 34*(2), 81–89.

Millard, G. (2005). Plagiarism: What to do about it. *International School, 1,* 15.

Montiel-Overall, P. (2005). A theoretical understanding of teacher and librarian collaboration (TLC). *School Libraries Worldwide, 11*(2), 24–48.

Monteil-Overall, P. (2008). Teacher and librarian collaboration: A qualitative study. *Library & Information Science Research, 30,* 145–155.

Moore, P. (2005). An analysis of information literacy education worldwide. *School Libraries Worldwide, 11*(2), 1–23.

Morley, K. (2004). Group 2: Second languages. In M. van Loo & K. Morley (Eds.), *Implementing the IB Diploma Programme: A practical manual for principals, IB coordinators, heads of department and teachers* (pp. 250–295). Cambridge, UK: Cambridge University Press.

Morley, K., Beverley, M., & Ruhil, A. (2004). Group 1: Language A1. In M. van Loo & K. Morley (Eds.), *Implementing the IB Diploma Programme: A practical manual for principals, IB coordinators, heads of department and teachers* (pp. 210–250). Cambridge, UK: Cambridge University Press.

Mueller, J., & Stefanics, P. (2004). Group 3: Information technology in a global society. In M. van Loo & K. Morley (Eds.), *Implementing the IB Diploma Programme: A practical manual for principals, IB coordinators, heads of department and teachers* (pp. 325–336). Cambridge, UK: Cambridge University Press.

Munro, J. (2003). The influence of student learning characteristics on progress through the extended essay, a component of the International Baccalaureate Diploma Programme. *Journal of Research in International Education, 2*(1), 5–24.

Oberg, D. (1995). *Principal support: What does it mean to teacher-librarians?* Retrieved from the University of Alberta website: http://www.alberta.ca/~doberg/prcsup.htm

Olen, S. (1995). Academic success and school library use. *School Libraries Worldwide, 1*(1), 69–79.

Paris, P.G. (2003). The International Baccalaureate: A case study on why students choose to do the IB. *International Education Journal, 4*(3), 232–243. Retrieved from http:www.flinders.edu.au/education/iej/articles/mainframe.htm

Peterson, A.D.C. (2003). *Schools across frontiers: The story of the International Baccalaureate and the United World Colleges* (2nd ed.). Chicago: Open Court.

Phillips, G., & Pound, T. (2003). *The baccalaureate: A model for curriculum reform*. London: Kogan Page.

Pollock, D. C., & Van Reken, R. (2009). *Third culture kids: The experience of growing up among worlds*. (2nd ed.). London: Nicholas Brealey Publishing.

Pound, T. (2006). *The International Baccalaureate diploma programme: An introduction for teachers and managers*. London: Routledge.

Pratt, D. (1994). *Curriculum planning: A handbook for professionals*. Fort Worth, TX: Harcourt Brace.

Qualifications and Curriculum Authority. (2003). *Report on comparability between GCE and International Baccalaureate examinations*. Retrieved from http://www.qca.org.uk/news/downloads/alevels_vs_ib.pdf

Rafste, E. T. (2003). *A place to learn or a place for pleasure? Pupils' use of the school library in Norway*. Retrieved from http://www.eric.ed.gov/ERICDocs/data/ericdocs2/content_storage_01/0000000b/80/23/4e/96.pdf

Rafste, E. T. (2005). A place to learn or a place for leisure: Pupils' use of the school library in Norway. *School Libraries Worldwide, 11*(1), 1–16.

Rataj-Worsnop, V. (2003). Pioneering the International Baccalaureate Diploma Programme in Hertfordshire [UK]. *Forum for Promoting 3–19 Comprehensive Education, 45, Pt. 2,* 47–52.

Riedling, A. M. (2004). *Information literacy: What does it look like in the school library media center?* Westport, CN: Libraries Unlimited.

Rowlands, I., & Nicholas, D. (2008). *Information behavior of the researcher of the future*. Retrieved from the British Library website: http://www.bl.uk/news/pdf/googlepackageii.pdf

Roys, N. K., & Brown, M. E. (2004). The ideal candidate for school library media specialist: Views from school administrators, library school faculty, and MLS students. *School Library Media Research, 7*. Retrieved from the American Library Association website: http:www.ala.org/ala/aasl/aaslpubsandjournals/slmrb/slmcontents/volume72004/candidate.htm

Sasaki, M. (1996). Who became kamikaze pilots, and how did they feel towards their suicide mission? *The Concord Review, 7*(1), 175–209.

Scott, L., & Owings, J. (2005). *School library media centers: Selected results from the education longitudinal study of 2002 (ELS:2002)*. Retrieved from the National Center for Education Statistics (U.S. Department of Education) website: http://nces.ed.gov/pubs2005/2005302.pdf

Scribner, M. E. (2000, November 28–30). *Notes for Diploma Program Librarians' Discussion: Resources for TOK, Extended Essay and other high level research*. Handout presented at International Baccalaureate Asia Pacific Librarians Workshop, Singapore.

Shaunessy, E., Suldo, S. M., Hardesty, R. B., & Shatter, E. J. (2006). School functioning and psychological well-being of International Baccalaureate and general education students: A preliminary examination. *Journal of Secondary Gifted Education, 17*(2), 78–89.

Shilling, C., & Cousins, F. (1990). Social use of the school library: The colonisation and regulation of educational space. *British Journal of Sociology of Education, 11*(4), 411–430.

Shoham, S., & Shemer-Shalman, Z. (2003). Territorial behaviour in the school library. *School Libraries Worldwide, 9*(2), 1–23.

Sjogren, C., & Vermey, E. G. (1986). The IB: Views from the American university. *International Quarterly, 4*(4), 26–29.

Smalley, T. N. (2004). College success: high school librarians make the difference. *Journal of Academic Librarianship, 30*(3), 193–198.

Snapper, G. (2006). Marked for life? Progression from the IBDP. In T. Pound (Ed.), *The International Baccalaureate diploma programme: An introduction for teachers and Managers* (pp. 171–188). London: Routledge.

Spahn, B.A. (2001). *America and the International Baccalaureate: Implementing the International Baccalaureate in the United States: a study of three schools.* Saxmundham, UK: John Catt Educational.

Spreadbury, H., & Spiller, D. (1999). *Survey of secondary school library users.* Loughborough, UK: Library & Information Statistics Unit, Loughborough University of Technology.

Stobie, T.D. (2005). To what extent do the Middle Years Programme and Diploma Programme of the International Baccalaureate Organization provide a coherent and consistent educational continuum? *International Schools Journal, 25*(1), 30–40.

Stobie, T. (2007). Coherence and consistency in international curricula: A study of the International Baccalaureate Diploma and Middle Years Programmes. In M. Hayden, J. Levy, & J. Thompson (Eds.), *Sage handbook of research in international education* (pp. 140–151). London: Sage Publications.

Streatfield, D., & Markless, S. (1994). *Invisible learning: The contribution of school libraries to teaching and learning.* London: British Library.

Taylor, L., Pogrebin, M., & Dodge, M. (2002). Advanced Placement—advanced pressures: Academic dishonesty among elite high school students. *Educational Studies, 33*(4), 403–432.

Taylor, M.L., & Porath, M. (2006). Reflections on the International Baccalaureate Program: Graduates' perspectives. *Journal of Secondary Gifted Education, 17*(3), 21–30.

Tekle, K. (2005). *The International Baccalaureate Diploma Programme (IBDP) at Katedralskolan, Uppsala: A study with emphasis on how the programme functions and on the teaching of geography.* (Unpublished master's thesis). Uppsala University, Sweden. Retrieved from http://www.katedral.se/~perssjn/ib

Tilke, A. (2009). *The impact of an international school library on the International Baccalaureate Diploma Programme: A constructivist grounded theory approach.* (Unpublished doctoral dissertation). Charles Sturt University, Australia.

Todd, R.J. (2003, August). *Learning in the information age school: Opportunities, outcomes and options.* Paper presented at the International Association of School Librarians conference, Durban, South Africa. Retrieved from the International Association of School Librarians website: http://www.iasl-slo.org/conference2003-virtualpap.html

Todd, R J. (2006). School libraries and evidence-based practice: An integrated approach to evidence. *School Libraries Worldwide, 12*(2), 31–37.

Todd, R.J., & Kuhlthau, C.C. (2005a). Student learning through Ohio school libraries, part 1: How effective school libraries help students. *School Libraries Worldwide, 11*(1), 63–88.

Todd, R.J., & Kuhlthau, C.C. (2005b). Student learning through Ohio school libraries, part 2: Faculty perceptions of effective school libraries, *School Libraries Worldwide, 11*(1), 89–110.

Turner, R. (2007). The use of independent school libraries in England and Wales. *School Librarian, 55*(1), 11–13, 15.

Vanderbrook, C.M. (2006). Intellectually gifted females and their perspectives of lived experience in the AP and IB programs. *Journal of Secondary Gifted Education, 17*(3), 133–148.

Van Reken, R., & Quick, T. (2010*). The global nomad's guide to university transition.* London, Summertime.

Voipio, V. (1993). Patent pending. *IB World, 4,* 14–15.

Walker, G. (2004). *International education and the International Baccalaureate.* Bloomington, IN: Phi Delta Kappa Educational Foundation.

Wallace, E. (2003). *The fine line: Communicating clearly in English in an international setting* (2nd ed.). St-Prex, Switzerland: Zidao Communication.

Wavell, C. (2004). *School librarians' understanding and descriptions of student learning in the school library.* (Unpublished master's thesis). Robert Gordon University, Aberdeen, Scotland. Retrieved from http://www.rgu.ac.uk/files/mastersinglespace2.doc

Wiggins, G. P. & McTighe, J. (2005). *Understanding by design.* Alexandria, VA: Association for Supervision and Curriculum Development.

Wiggins, G. P. & McTighe, J. (2007). *Schooling by design: Mission, action and achievement.* Alexandria, VA: Association for Supervision and Curriculum Development.

Williams, D. (2006). *Support for evidence based practice in teaching: The role of the school librarian?* Retrieved from the Robert Gordon University website: http://www.rgu.ac.uk/files/IALS%20paper%2016%20Jun.doc

Williams, D., & Wavell, C. (2001). *The impact of the school library resource centre on learning: A report on research conducted for Resource: the Council for Museums, Archives and Libraries.* Aberdeen, Scotland: The Robert Gordon University.

Williams, D., & Wavell, C. (2002, July). Learning and the school library resource centre. In D. Singh, A. Abdullah, D. Abdullah, S. Fonseka, & B. de Rozario (Eds.), *School Libraries for a Knowledge Society: Proceedings of the 31st Annual Conference of the International Association of School Librarianship and the Sixth International Forum on Research in School Librarianship* (pp. 77–90). Seattle, WA: International Association of School Librarians.

Williams, D., & Wavell, C. (2006). *Information literacy in the classroom: Secondary school teachers' conceptions. Final report on research funded by Society for Educational Studies.* Retrieved from the Aberdeen Business School/Robert Gordon University website: http://www.rgu.ac.uk/files/ACF4DAA.pdf

Williams, D., Wavell, C., & Coles, L. (2001). *Impact of school library services on achievement and learning: Critical literature review of the impact of school library services on achievement and learning to inform the work of the DfES Task Group set up to implement actions contained in the government's response to "Empowering the Learning Community."* Aberdeen, Scotland: The Robert Gordon University.

Williamson, K., McGregor, J., Archibald, A., & Sullivan, J. (2007). Information seeking and use by secondary students: The link between good practice and the avoidance of plagiarism. *School Library Media Research, 10.* Retrieved from the American Library Association website: http://www.ala.org/ala/aasl/aaslpubsandjournals/slmrb/slmrcontents/volume10/williamson_informationseeking.cfm

Wright, D., & Christine, R. (2006). The sixth-form library without walls. In G. Dubber (Ed.), *Sixth sense: The sixth form and the LRC* (pp. 18–22). Swindon, UK: School Library Association.

Yip, T.W. (2000). An analysis of the status quo: The International Baccalaureate Diploma Programme and the empowerment of students. *International Schools Journal, 19*(2), 37–47.

INDEX

A1 language group, 22–23
AASL. *See* American Association of School Librarians
Ab initio language, 23
Abstracts, 42–43
Academically weak students, 75
Academic honesty, 9, 44, 72; defined, 54; IB academic honesty document, 54–55; modeling and promoting, 29–30; school academic honesty policy, 55
Accountability, 87, 94
Acronyms, 6, 7, 30
Administrators, 2, 13, 52, 73–75, 77, 80, 88, 90; stakeholders as, 4–5. *See also* Libraries, IBDP administrator use of
Advisory Committee, 85
Advocacy, 4
Aide memoire, 45
Alexander Technique, 69
American Association of School Librarians (AASL), 3
Areas of Knowledge, 27, 29, 30–31
Arts, study of (group 6 of the subject matrix), 25–26
Asian literature, 14–15
Assessed coursework (internal assignments), 21. *See also* Subject matrix
Australia, 3, 4, 33, 76, 87
Australian Council for Educational Research (Coates, Rosicka, & MacMahon-Ball), 33
Australian School Library Association, 58

Austria, 36
Authority, 27
Authorization process, 11–13, 19
Authorization teams, 13, 14

Baccalaureate, defining, 3
"Back to school night," 44
Banned books, 56
Belief, 28
Bibliographies, 18, 29, 40–41, 44, 46, 51–52, 55–56, 63, 71–73, 84, 89
Bilingualism, 14–15, 23
Brain gym, 69
British Columbia, IBDP research project at, 12–13
Buildings and facilities, 5-year re-authorization and, 12–13

Canada, 87
Canteens, studying in, 89
Cardiff, Wales, United Kingdom, 16
CAS. *See* Creativity, action, and service
Case study of an IBDP school library, 88–92
Center for Evaluation and Education Policy at Indiana University, 50
Certificate option, 10, 60, 75–76
Charles Stuart University, Australia, 2
Chartered Institute of Library and Information Professionals (CILIP) (London), 2–3
China, 1, 23

CILIP. *See* Chartered Institute of Library and Information Professionals (London)

Citation, 34, 36–41, 46, 51–52, 55–56, 61, 64, 72, 89

Collaboration between librarians and teachers, 28–31, 46, 56, 69, 71–72, 78–80, 82–83, 94–95

Collection development policy, 56

Collections: discrete, 31, 66; international mindedness and, 93; languages and, 82; of previous years' extended essays, 46; providing up-to-date, 82–83; for Theory of Knowledge (TOK) in libraries, 28–29, 31–32

Collusion, 55

Communication, teacher/librarian, 82–83, 94–95. *See also* Collaboration; Liaison between librarians and teachers

Computer sciences studies (group 5 of the subject matrix), 25

Computer use in libraries, 60–61, 64, 90

Concluding projects, 9, 16, 56. *See also* Extended essays

Concord Review, 24, 35

Concurrency of learning, 94

Conferences, 16

Constructivism, 30, 31, 75, 88

Constructivist pedagogy, 59

Consumer-focused school library: environment of, 84; pedagogical use of, 82–84; practical strategies for the librarian, 84–85; uses of libraries/librarians, 81–82

Content-rich lecture style teaching, 49

Content-rich transmitted curriculum environment, 75

Content-transfer experiences, 74–75

Continuum approach, 9, 16

Continuum of skills development, 47, 55. *See also* Learner profile

Continuum Schools, 9

Continuum workshop model, 17

Coordinators (IBDP), 17, 19, 30, 69; for academic honesty, 55; for creativity, action, and service (CAS), 32; for the extended essay (EE), 33–34, 38, 45–46

Coordinator's Notes (IBDP), 17, 19, 25

Core collections, for Theory of Knowledge (TOK), 29

Core requirements, 5, 10, 21. *See also* Creativity, action, and service (CAS); Extended essay (EE); Subject matrix; Theory of Knowledge (TOK)

Creative thinking, 1, 29

Creativity, action, and service (CAS), 10, 21, 32, 44, 60, 62–63, 78

Critical thinking, 1, 62, 84; essay titles and, 28; extended essay experience and, 39; Theory of Knowledge and, 27, 29

Cultures: cultural viewpoints in library collections, 28; intercultural communication, 29; internationalism and, 14–15

Curriculum, 6, 95; global, 1, 22; inquiry and, 5; role statements and, 87; Standard C of *Programme Standards and Practices* (IB), 14, 94; time for the extended essay (EE), 42. *See also* Subject matrix

Curriculum and assessment center (IBCA), 16, 91

Data, 4

Databases, use of, 35, 39–40, 45–46, 59, 67, 90

Debate, 29

Development planning, 91

Dewey Decimal Classification, 15, 29, 30, 31

Didactic teaching practices, 58

Digital natives, 59

Diploma Programme (DP), 1–2, 74–75, 91–95. *See also* International Baccalaureate Diploma Programme (IBDP)

"Diploma Programme Evaluation" (IB), 11

Diploma Programme, The: A Basis for Practice (IBDP), 9, 18

Diploma requirements, 21, 60

Diploma students, 11, 72. *See also* Libraries, IBDP student use of; Students

Direct quotations, 40

Discrete collections, 31, 66

Dual-language texts, 82

EAL. *See* English as an additional language

EBP. *See* Evidence-based practice

Economics studies, 23

EE. *See* Extended essays

English, types of, 15

English as an additional language (EAL), 75

English as a second language (ESL), 30, 75

Environment of libraries, 81, 84

ESL. *See* English as a second language

Essay Guide for examinations, abstracts, 42

Ethics, 30, 56. *See also* Academic honesty

Ethnography, 4–5

Europe, 16, 77

Evaluating libraries, 77; authorization and re-authorization processes, 11–13; *Guide to Programme Evaluation* (IB), 11–13, 18

Evidence-based practice research (EBP), 4, 7, 79, 94

Examiners, 16, 17

Exhibition (PYP), 16

Expatriates, 1, 9

Experimental sciences studies (group 4 of the subject matrix), 24

Extended essays (EE), 9–10, 12, 16–17, 21, 32–46, 52, 55, 59; the abstract, 42–43; aspects of, 39; bibliographies, 40–41; citations, 40–41; curriculum time for, 42; formulating a question for, 41; good practices modeling by librarians, 41; grading, 33; IB guide to (available on the OCC), 33; length of, 33; libraries/librarians' role, 34–35, 45–46, 60–67, 73–76, 78–79, 89–91, 94; paraphrasing, 40; parts of, 33; presentation about the library's role, 38–42; quotations, 40; research about, 33–34; supporting students in their EE needs, 43–44; time guideline for completing (IB), 33; titles of, 35–38, 41–42; using student experiences, 41; working with the IBDP coordinator and EE supervisors, 45

Facilities: 5-year re-authorization process and, 12–13; managing, 29

Final examinations, 74

Five-year re-authorization process, 11–13

Formal examinations, 21

Freedom of information, 56

Freerunning, 28

Free time, 26–27

Full-text databases, 46

G10 (grade 10), 76

G11 (grade 11) library use, 30, 61–66, 69, 75, 89

G12 (grade 12) library use, 30, 51, 61–66, 69, 75, 76, 89

Geography studies, 24

Gifted students, 10–11, 75

Global curriculum, 1, 22

Globalization, 14

Global reading lists, 14–15

Glogster, 48, 56

Good practices, 3, 35, 41, 49, 83, 89

Google, 18

Grading: for the extended essay (EE), 33; for the subject matrix, 21. *See also* Marks

Grounded theories, 4–5, 59, 68, 78–80. *See also* Libraries, IBDP administrator use of; Libraries, IBDP student use of; Libraries, IBDP teacher use of; Research Groups in the subject matrix. *See* Subject matrix

Guidelines, 4, 87–88. *See also Guide to Programme Evaluation* (IB); Role statements of the IBDP libraries; *Programme Standards and Practices* (IB)

Guide to Programme Evaluation (IB), 11–13, 18

High-content courses, 72–74

Higher level (HL) subjects, 22

Historical writings, 12

History studies, 23–24

HL. *See* Higher level (HL) subjects

Homework, 89

Honesty document (IB), 54–55

Honor codes, 44

Hours of operation of libraries, 29, 85

Hypotheses, 4, 33

IB. *See* International Baccalaureate (Organization)

IB(O). *See* International Baccalaureate (Organization)

IBA. *See* International Baccalaureate Americas

IB and Higher Education: Developing Policy for the IB Diploma Program Examinations (IBO), 21

IBAP. *See* International Baccalaureate Asia Pacific (region of the IB)

IBAPLIS. *See* International Baccalaureate Asia-Pacific Library and Information Specialists (IBAPLIS) group

IBCA. *See* Curriculum and assessment center

IBDP. *See* International Baccalaureate Diploma Programme

IBEAM. *See* International Baccalaureate Europe, Africa, Middle East

"IB-Extended Essay Procrastination" video on YouTube, 46

IB Global Policy and Research Team, 50

iBooks, 60

IB Prepared: Approach Your Assessment the IB Way—Extended Essay (IB), 43

IBVC. *See* International Baccalaureate Virtual Community

IB World (IB), 18–19, 35, 91, 93

IB World Schools, 1–2, 13

IB World Schools Yearbook (IB), 18

Iceberg model, 15

ICT. *See* Information and communications technology

IL. *See* Information literacy

Impact studies, 3–4, 4, 7, 60, 66, 74, 77–78, 88

Implementing the IB Diploma Programme: A Practical Manual for Principals, IB Coordinators, Heads of Department and Teachers (van Loo and Morley), 17

Independent learning and research, 33–34, 58, 62, 73–74, 91

India, 1

Individuals and societies (group 3 of the subject matrix), 23–24

Information and communications technology (ICT), 3, 5–6, 12, 17, 24, 61–66, 76, 78, 87

Information literacy (IL), 6, 58, 72, 77, 84, 87–88, 94; results of the IBDP library study in relation to information literacy, 51–54

Information specialists, librarians as, 5–6

Information technology (IT) facilities, 69

Information technology in a global society (ITGS), 24

Input measures, 87, 94

Inquiry, 1–2, 46, 74, 85; as a curriculum stance, 5, 81; essay titles and, 28

Inquiry-centered uses of libraries/librarians, 81–82

Intercultural communication development, 29

Internal assignments (assessed coursework), 21

International Baccalaureate (IB), 1; Association of Japan and Korea, 17; concluding projects, 16; *Coordinator's Notes,* 17; examiners in, 16; headquarters (Geneva, Switzerland), 16; IB academic honesty document, 54–55; IB Librarians Continuum wiki, 18; IB Virtual Community (IBVC), 17; *Implementing the IB Diploma Programme: A Practical Manual for Principals, IB Coordinators, Heads of Department and Teachers* (van Loo and Morley), 17; *International Baccalaureate Diploma Programme: An Introduction for Teachers and Managers* (Pound), 17, 43; Mid-Atlantic, 17; Mission Statement, 15–16, 18, 93; moderators on the OCC, 17; *Programme Standards and Practices,* 11, 14, 18, 92–95; regions of, 16; role statements for IBDP libraries and, 87–88; Standard A (philosophy and international mindedness), 14, 93; Standard B (organization), 14, 93–94; Standard C (curriculum), 14, 94; website, 1, 6, 11, 18; World Schools, 1–2, 13; workshops of, 16, 19, 28, 30, 34, 71, 82, 85

International Baccalaureate (IB) World Schools, 1–2, 13

International Baccalaureate Americas (region of the IB) (IBA), 1–2, 16

International Baccalaureate Asia Pacific (region of the IB) (IBAP), 2, 16, 17

International Baccalaureate Asia Pacific Library and Information Specialists (IBAPLIS) group, 2

International Baccalaureate Diploma Programme: An Introduction for Teachers and Managers (Pound), 17, 43

International Baccalaureate Diploma Programme (IBDP); authorization and re-authorization, 11–13; background and issues concerning, 1–7, 9–11; benefits of, 10–11; certificate option, 10; curriculums, 9–11; *Guide to Programme Evaluation,* 11–13; internationalism and language in the, 14–15; library technology and, 5–6; model, 3, 10; narrative of one school's relationship with the library/librarian, 88–92; *Programme Standards and Practices* (IB), 11, 14, 18, 92–95; results of the IBDP library study in relation to information literacy, 51–54; role statements and, 87–88; school libraries' impact on, 3–4. *See also* Creativity, action, and service (CAS); Extended essays (EE); "Libraries" entries; Subject matrix; Theory of Knowledge (TOK)

International Baccalaureate Europe, Africa, Middle East (IBEAM), 16, 91

International Baccalaureate Virtual Community (IBVC), 17

Internationalism, 9, 18; defining for libraries, 7; IBDP language and, 14–15;

relevance of, 5. *See also* International mindedness
International literature, 5
International mindedness, 5, 14–15, 18, 93. *See also* Internationalism
Internet: academic honesty and, 55; use of in libraries, 40, 58–67, 72–73, 89–90. *See also* Websites
Internet-searching skills, 53
Issues of knowledge, 27
IT. *See* Information technology (IT) facilities
ITGS. *See* Information technology in a global society

Japan, extended essay titles of an international school in, 37–38
Jargon, 6, 7, 30
Journal of Research in International Education, 15

K-12 international education, 9
K-12 library use, 91
Key terms (IB/TOK language or jargon), 27–28
Knower(s), 28, 30
Knowledge class, 29
Knowledge management skills, 29
Knowledge Quest, 18

Language A1, 22–23, 36
Language A2, 23
Language B, 23
Language development, 28; group 1 in the subject matrix (first language study), 22–23; group 2 in the subject matrix (study in second or third languages), 14, 23; IB documents about, 18; provisions for in libraries, 15
Larger-scale studies, 4
Learner Profile (IB), 82
Learner profile (LP), 9, 72; descriptors for, 48; elements of, 3, 47–48, 93–94; importance of, 47; libraries/librarians' role, 48–51; results of the IBDP library study in relation to information literacy, 51–54; skills and qualities of, 49–50
Learning in a Language Other Than Mother Tongue in IB Programmes (IB), 14
Lecture-style teaching format, 74
Liaison, between librarians and teachers, 28–31, 46, 56, 69, 71–72, 78–80, 82–83, 94–95

Librarians: collaboration with teachers, 28–31, 46, 56, 69, 71–72, 78–80, 82–83, 94–95; defined by teachers, 72; defining, 3; as disciplinarians, 57; IBDP role statements and, 87–88; information technology in a global society (ITGS) and, 24; inquiry-centered uses of, 81–82; learner profile (LP) and, 48–51, 55–56; memo technique in grounded theory, 78; narrative of an IBDP school, 88–92; *Programme Standards and Practices* (IB), 14, 92–95; role of in academic honesty, 55; role of in extended essays (EE), 34–35, 38–42, 45–46; role of in the subject matrix (IBDP), 26–27; role of in Theory of Knowledge (TOK), 27–31; stakeholders as, 4–5; strategies for, 6–7, 18–19, 32, 46, 55–56, 68–69, 80, 84–85; students' view of, 79; teachers' view of, 72, 78–79. *See also* Libraries
"Librarians, Counselors and Non-teaching Staff" (*School Guide to the Authorization*), 13
Libraries: defining, 3; evaluating, 85; hours of operation, 85; IBDP re-authorization and, 12–13; IBDP role statements and, 87–88; impact of on the International Baccalaureate Diploma Programme (IBDP), 3–4; inquiry-centered uses of, 81–82; language provisions in, 15; location of, 85; mission statements/policy, 84; naming, 81, 84; narrative of an IBDP school library, 88–92; *Programme Standards and Practices* (IB), 14, 92–95; results of the IBDP library study in relation to information literacy, 51–54; social good of, 4; socializing in, 57, 59–62, 67, 89–90, staffing, 85; Theory of Knowledge (TOK) collections in, 31–32; Theory of Knowledge (TOK) support in, 28–29. *See also* Consumer-focused school library; Librarians
Libraries, IBDP administrator use of, 73–75, 77, 80
Libraries, IBDP student use of, 57–69; activities in, 60–61; comparison of G11 and G12, 63–66; G11 students, 61–66, 89; G12 students, 61–66, 89; helpfulness of the library before starting IBDP, 68; impressions of students who had finished the IBDP program, 62–63; Internet use, 58–67; older student needs, 57–59; perceptions of the library, 67–68; for

socializing, 57, 59–62, 67, 89–90; strategies for the librarian and, 68–69; student's view of, 78–79, 90; studying, 57–69; textbooks and, 58, 63–64; what it looks like, 66–67. *See also* Students

Libraries, IBDP teacher use of, 71–80; collaboration with librarians, 28–31, 46, 56, 69, 71–72, 78–80, 82–83, 94–95; evaluating, 77; high-content courses and, 72–73; impact on teachers, 77–78; library roles and subject content, 75; library use in class time (limited), 72; modeling library usage, 73, 76–77; personal use, 89; study halls and, 72, 75; teachers' view of librarians, 72, 78–79. *See also* Teachers

Library and information science (LIS), 3, 4, 51, 57–58, 77, 90; library anxiety study, 59; qualitative studies and, 5; role statements and, 87–88; study of information sources, 40

Library anxiety, 59

Library catalogs, 45, 61–64, 90

Lifelong learners, 16, 83

LIS. *See* Library and information science

Listservs, 2, 14, 17, 18, 30

Literary criticism, 12, 22

Literature, internationalism and, 5, 14–15

Location of the library, 85

LP. *See* Learner profile

Marks, requirements for diploma, 21. *See also* Grading

Mathematics courses (group 5 of the subject matrix), 25

Mechanical skills, 84

Media, 5, 31, 40

Memo technique in grounded theory, 78

Mentoring, 29

Middle Years Programme (MYP), 9, 17, 68; personal project, 16

Minority students, 10

Mission statements (IB), 15–16, 18, 84, 93

Modeling: academic honesty, 29; knowledge management skills, 29; library usage, 73, 76–77, 83–84, 91–92, 94; understanding and acceptance of different viewpoints, 29

Models: baccalaureate-style education, 3; iceberg model, 15; inquiry or research, 5

Moderators, 17

Mother tongue library collections, 15, 18, 29, 82

Multiple-ability year groups, 10

MYP. *See* Middle Years Programme

Naming of libraries, 81, 84

Narratives, 5

Negotiation, 94

Netherlands, 76

New Scientist, 24

New Zealand, 33, 87

North America, 4, 5, 16

Norway, 76

Observation exercise, 80

OCC. *See* Online Curriculum Center

Ohio, 76

Older students, 5, 30, 57–69, 89. *See also* Libraries, IBDP student use of

One-off meetings, 19

Online catalog, 67

Online Curriculum Center (OCC), 6, 11, 17, 32; abstracts, 42; academic honesty document, 54, 56; creativity, action, and service (CAS) requirements, 32; essay titles from an international school in Vienna, Austria, 36; IB guide to the extended essay (EE), 33; learner profile document, 56; syllabuses and, 22; Theory of Knowledge (TOK) and, 31; website, 18

Online groups, 2

Online help/support service, 46

Organization (Standard B of *Programme Standards and Practices*) (IB), 14, 93–94

Outcomes, 87, 94–95

Paradigm, 28

Paraphrasing, 40

Parents, 13

Pedagogical use of the library, 49, 59, 71, 73, 76–77, 80, 82–84, 90; defining, 82–83; developing, 83–84. *See also* Collaboration between librarians and teachers; Liaison between librarians and teachers

Personal project (MYP), 16

Philosophy (Standard A of *Programme Standards and Practices*) (IB), 14, 93

Plagiarism, 30, 39, 44, 50–51, 55–56, 72, 84

Post-extended essay period case study, 59

Practices. *See Programme Standards and Practices* (IB)

Pre-authorization funding, 13

Pretertiary education, 3
Primary Years Programme (PYP), 9, 17; exhibition project, 16
Principals, 80
Print sources, 40
Process and outcomes, 87, 94–95
Professional development, 71, 73, 93
Programme, spelling of word, 6
Programme Standards and Practices (IB), 11, 14, 18, 92–95; aims for, 94–95; Standard A (philosophy and international mindedness), 14, 93; Standard B (organization), 14, 93–94; Standard B2 (library role), 93–94; Standard C (curriculum), 14, 94
Project Information Literacy, 58
PYP. *See* Primary Years Programme

Qualification and Curriculum Authority (U.K.), 33
Qualitative methods: for library and information science (LIS), 5; vs. quantitative methods, 4–5
Quality assurance, 94
Quantitative methods, 66; vs. qualitative methods, 4–5
Questioning skills, 29
Questions, forming for the extended essay (EE), 41
Quotations, 40

Reason, 28
Re-authorization process, 11–13, 19
Referencing conventions, 46, 89. *See also* Bibliographies; Citation; Extended essays
Referencing skills, 34
Reflection process, 5
Relaxation classes, 69
Research: evidence-based, 4; grounded theory methodology, 4–5; independent, 33–34, 58, 73–74; interviewing students and staff about the library, 80; learner profile, 49–54; qualitative methods vs. quantitative methods to, 4–5; resource implications of the IBDP and libraries, 12–13; results of the IBDP library study in relation to information literacy, 51–54; workshops for, 34. *See also* Extended essays (EE); Grounded theories
Research-based essays. *See* Extended essays (EE)

Research skills development, 29, 50
Research skills study, 51–54
Resource management, 29, 71–72, 78, 82–83
Resource research, 12–13
Role models. *See* Modeling
Role statements of the IBDP libraries, 4, 57, 87–88
Rubric, 45

Scaffolding, 10, 29, 49, 59, 75
School Guide to the Authorization (IB), 13
School librarians. *See* Librarians
School libraries. *See* Libraries
Scientific American, 24
Search terms, 29
Seed funding, 13
Self-discovery, 1
Self-evaluation, 11
Self-help webgroups, 17
Self-motivation, 52
Self-study process, 11, 19
Sense perception, 28
Skills, learner profile, 49–50
SL. *See* Standard level (SL) subjects
Smaller-scale studies, 4
Soap box graffiti board, 29
Social good of libraries, 4
Socialization aspect of library use, 57, 59–62, 67
Societies studies (group 3 of the subject matrix), 23–24
South Africa, 77
Stakeholders, 4–5, 13
Standard level (SL) subjects, 22
Standards and practices. *See Programme Standards and Practices* (IB)
Standards for the 21st Century Learner (American Association of School Librarians, 2007, 2009), 87
Stress management, 63, 69
Student lounges, libraries as, 89–90
Students: older, 5, 57–59; stakeholders as, 4–5; support for their extended essays (EE), 43–44; view of librarians/libraries, 78–79, 90. *See also* Libraries, IBDP student use of
Studies: information literacy, 51–54; library anxiety, 50; qualitative vs. quantitative, 4–5. *See also* Libraries, IBDP administrator use of; Libraries, IBDP student use of; Libraries, IBDP teacher use of; Research

Study hall (study times), 26–27, 65–66,
    72–73, 75, 78–79, 89–90
Studying. *See* Libraries, IBDP student use
    of; Study hall (study times)
Study times. *See* Study hall
Subject-based resources, 73
Subject documentation, 52, 77
Subject faculties, 6, 89
Subject groups. *See* Subject matrix
Subject matrix: background, 21–22; group
    1: language A1 group, 22–23; group
    2: second language group (language *ab
    initio*, language B, language A2), 23,
    75; group 3: individuals and society,
    23–24; group 4: experimental sciences,
    24, 36, 75; group 5: math and computer
    sciences, 25, 75; group 6: the arts,
    25–26; higher level (HL), 22; librarians'
    role, 26–27; options within, 22; standard
    level (SL), 22; study times or study hall,
    26–27
Supervisors, extended essays (EE) and,
    44–46, 55
Syllabuses, 5, 22, 30

TCK. *See* Third-culture kids
Teacher-librarian, 94–95
Teachers: collaboration with librarians,
    28–31, 46, 56, 69, 71–72, 78–80,
    82–83, 94–95; personal use of libraries,
    89; stakeholders as, 4–5; of Theory of
    Knowledge (TOK), 28–31; view of
    librarians, 72, 78–79. *See also* Libraries,
    IBDP teacher use of
Team teaching, 94. *See also* Collaboration
    between librarians and teachers; Liaison
    between librarians and teachers
Technology: and the International
    Baccalaureate Diploma Programme
    (IBDP) library, 5–6; in libraries, 6,
    58–59, 78. *See also* Computer use in
    libraries; Internet; Websites
"Template for a Plagiarism Policy: Goals of
    an Ethics Policy" (Noodletools.com), 56
Terminology, 3, 6–7, 32; key terms (IB/
    TOK), 27–28
Tertiary education, 9, 33, 44, 50, 59
Test scores, 4
Textbooks, 58, 63–64, 72, 74–75, 78–79,
    89–90
Theory of Knowledge (TOK), 2, 10, 17,
    21; essay, 32, 52; inquiry and critical
    thinking, 28; key terms, 27–28; a library
    collection for, 31–32; library support

and use, 28–29, 60, 63–65, 75–76, 78;
    teachers' role, 30–31
Theory of Knowledge (TOK) circle,
    27–28, 30
*Theory of Knowledge Guide for First
    Examinations 2008* (available on the
    OCC), 27
Third-culture kids (TCK), 14–15
Time management skills, 39, 50–52,
    62–65, 69, 72, 74, 89
Titles: of extended essays (EE), 35–38; tips
    for formulating for the extended essay
    (EE), 41–42
TOK. *See* Theory of Knowledge
*Towards a Continuum of International
    Education* (IB), 14, 15, 18
Trilingualism, 23
Truth, 27
Turnitin.com, 55
Tutoring, 29, 44, 46, 56

Understanding by Design concept
    (Wiggins and McTighe), 5
United Kingdom, 3, 4, 75, 76, 87;
    Qualification and Curriculum Authority,
    33
United Kingdom Library Association.
    See Chartered Institute of Library and
    Information Professionals (CILIP)
    (London)
United Kingdom National Foundation for
    Educational Research, 10
United States, 4, 12
Unpacking questions, 29
URLs, 6

Virtual classroom space, 29
Vocational subject areas, 10

*Walking Two Moons: Crossing Borders with
    International Literature* (Royce), 18
Ways of Knowing (WoK), 27, 30–31
Web 2.0 applications, 69
Websites: Asia-Pacific region wiki, 16;
    citing, 41; International Baccalaureate
    (IB), 1, 6, 18; Knowledge Quest, 18;
    Librarians Continuum wiki, 18; Online
    Curriculum Center (OCC), 18; student-
    led, 46; "Template for a Plagiarism
    Policy: Goals of an Ethics Policy"
    (Noodletools.com), 56; Turnitin.com,
    55; United World College of South-East
    Asia, Singapore, 15; unofficial, 32, 46
WoK. *See* Ways of Knowing

Workshops: IB library workshops, 19, 28, 30, 95; IB teacher workshops, 16, 71, 82, 85; on research, 34; TOK training workshops, 30

World literature, 14–15; study of, 22–23

World Schools (IB), 1–2, 13

Written policy statements, 7. *See also* Role statements of the IBDP libraries

Yahoo, 18

ABOUT THE AUTHOR

ANTHONY TILKE is head of library at the International School of Amsterdam in the Netherlands, and has worked with the International Baccalaureate Diploma Programme (IBDP) for over 10 years. His PhD thesis was on the impact of an international school library on the IBDP. He is the author of several titles on school librarianship that have been published in the United Kingdom.

33079395R10084

Made in the USA
San Bernardino, CA
23 April 2016